Praise for

Umbrella Guide to Bicycling The Oregon Coast

"Take time to enjoy the spectacular ride along the Oregon Coast. And take this guide to help you discover the region's history and local color. If you've never been to the area, you'd be foolish not to consult this guide. Remarkable detail!"

Jim Canton, Publisher, *Oregon Cycling*

"A thoroughly researched and vividly descriptive guide. I can't wait to hop on my bike and explore the area."

Howard Stone, author of *Short Bike Rides in Greater Boston and Central Massachusetts*, and other regional bicycling guides

"This guide's fascinating historical perspective, and the regional insights into the land and the people, provide a whole new dimension for anyone bicycling the Oregon Coast. Cody is also very thorough in describing road conditions, degree of difficulty, and where to find services along each part of the route."

Kirk Welfelt, Owner, Beckwith Bicycles Store, Portland, OR

"Robin Cody's enthusiasm for the area is contagious. The historical detail offered is so fascinating that even those bikers who generally 'rush headlong down the road' may slow down for the lighthouses, fishing villages, and seascapes that are so colorfully described. We will definitely be packing this book in our panniers when we head for the Oregon Coast."

Elizabeth & Charlie Skinner, authors of *Bicycling the Blue Ridge*

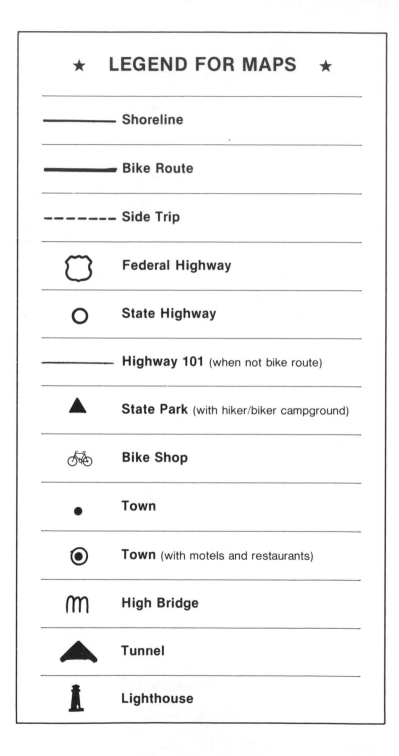

★ LEGEND FOR MAPS ★

——————— Shoreline

━━━━━━━ Bike Route

- - - - - - - Side Trip

⬡ **Federal Highway**

○ **State Highway**

——————— **Highway 101** (when not bike route)

▲ **State Park** (with hiker/biker campground)

🚲 **Bike Shop**

• **Town**

◉ **Town** (with motels and restaurants)

ɱ **High Bridge**

▲ **Tunnel**

🗼 **Lighthouse**

UMBRELLA GUIDE TO
BICYCLING THE
OREGON COAST

by

Robin Cody

T.M.

UMBRELLA
BOOKS

ISBN: 0-914143-25-5

Published by:

Umbrella Books
A Division of Harbor View Publications Group, Inc.
440 Tucker Ave., PO Box 1460
Friday Harbor, WA 98250-1460

Table of Contents

Umbrella Guides to the Pacific Northwest

Jerome K. Miller, Series Editor

Umbrella Guide to Friday Harbor & San Juan Island

Umbrella Guide to Bicycling the Oregon Coast

Umbrella Guide to Inland Empire

Umbrella Guide to Washington Lighthouses

Forthcoming Titles

Umbrella Guide to Glacier & Waterton National Parks

Umbrella Guide to Northwest Hot Springs

Umbrella Guide to San Juan Island Beaches

Umbrella Guide to Inland Empire Antique Stores

Umbrella Guide to Victoria B.C.

Praise for The Umbrella Guide Series

"Exploring the Northwest will be more enjoyable with the help of these guides. The excellent Umbrella Guide series offers in-depth coverage of areas and subjects that are unusual and offbeat — and interesting."

Archie Satterfield, author of *The Seattle Guidebook* and former newspaper and magazine editor

Bicyclers assume responsibility for their own safety when they take a bike trip. No guidebook can warn bikers of every hazard or anticipate all the dangers of terrain, road conditions, traffic, weather and the abilities of individual bikers. Keep informed about current weather and road conditions, and have a safe, enjoyable trip.

Introduction

"Rugged" and "scenic" are the words most often associated with the Oregon Coast. The coastline has a rich variety of rocky headlands, offshore seastacks, quiet coves and inlets and breakers crashing against wide, sandy beaches. Vast stretches of the coast have been preserved as state parks or have been otherwise protected from development. Bikers can see coastal forests in their natural state and appreciate the rough forces of sea, wind and continental shift that are still battling, still forming this broken and beautiful seascape.

The coast is also dotted with places of historical and human interest. The Oregon Coast has its sacred Indian sites and its capes and river mouths explored and named by early seafarers. Coastal towns grew up around gold prospectors, timber barons, fishermen and cheesemakers. Museums, shipwrecks, lighthouses, bridges and jetties all have stories to tell about a land that until three or four generations ago was effectively isolated from the world of hard-surface roads and commercial development.

This guide was written to make it easier for bikers to find and appreciate the Oregon Coast's natural and unnatural wonders. It's for bikers who are not in a hurry. It's for bikers who want to experience the flavor of the place rather than rushing headlong down the road. You are encouraged to slow down for the Indian legends, natural landmarks and pioneer stories that introduce the character of the land and its people.

The Route

The Oregon Coast Bike Route goes from Astoria, in the northwest corner of the state, to the California border. For most of the way, the bike route is the shoulder of U.S. Highway 101. A shoulder stripe separates bike traffic from motor vehicles, and in most places the shoulder is wide and well-maintained. Oregon has set aside one percent of its state highway funds for bikeways throughout the state, and the coastal route is one of the chief beneficiaries. Nevertheless there are brief stretches — including two quarter-mile tunnels — where Highway 101 narrows and bikers must exercise extreme caution. Occasionally the bike route leaves Highway 101 in favor of scenic and lightly-traveled county roads that lack shoulder stripes.

The 370-mile route is extremely hilly, but not mountainous. At the pace we recommend, the route is strenuous, not exhausting. The Oregon Coast Bike Route never exceeds an elevation of 750 feet. Whenever it rises, it quickly seeks sea level again. The judgments in this book about "steep hills" or "tough climbs" were formed by a 46-year-old and his wife traveling on Schwinn Miradas loaded with camping gear, which suggests that just about any experienced biker, in decent shape, can do it. Physically, that is.

The coastal bike route is not for beginners, not for kids, not for anybody with a short attention span. The chief danger is traffic. Highway 101 is the primary commercial and tourist route up and down the coast. In most places it is the only route. Bikers share the road with log trucks, chip trucks, delivery vans and the ubiquitous recreational vehicles. Highway 101 demands biking courtesy and constant attention to safe biking practices. Obey traffic signals. Signal every intention to turn. Ride single file, and stay in the bike lane. Dismount and walk the bike on sidewalks across the tall, windy bridges.

Following these common-sense safety procedures will keep bikers out of the way of the log truckers. The logging season is short, and it overlaps the biking season on the Oregon Coast. Truckers are in a hurry to make a living, but they are professional drivers who know what they are doing. They give safe bikers enough room.

RV drivers, on the other hand, may not have a complete and accurate idea of how much road their rigs take up. Give an RV driver the right-of-way at turnouts and viewpoints; he's bigger, and he has paid more to get here than you have. For every horror story a biker can tell about rude RV drivers, they can probably tell one about careless bikers who ride tandem or don't stay in the bike lane.

The Pace

This guidebook divides the coastal bike route into nine chapters, each of which ends at a coastal town with full tourist facilities. Each chapter covers from twenty-three to fifty-six miles, with an average of forty-one miles. Occasionally we lapse into calling these chapters "days," because a day is about how long we think it would take to stop and poke around at the places of interest in each chapter, as well as to bike from its beginning to end. Biker-racers can easily cover the coastal route in much less time than nine days. On the other hand, there's a lot to see and explore. Those who are really curious might take the coast at an even slower pace than nine days, and not be bored. Biker-campers will want to note the campsites marked on the maps and in the text, and make their own adjustments.

Food and Lodging

On the Oregon Coast a biker is seldom far from a town that has a wide range of restaurants, grocery stores and motels, a bike shop, a laundromat, a post office, a bank and whatever else a biker might need. The larger towns have visitor information centers, so this guide does not duplicate their services by picking out places to stay and eat. We do identify a few hotels and restaurants that are unusual or propitiously located, and we mention a country grocery store here and there. These exceptions are not meant to slight the many fine options for food and lodging in more populated areas.

This guide identifies the Oregon State Parks that have hiker/biker campsites. These are the best places for bikers with camping gear to stop for the night. Some of the campsites are strikingly beautiful, pristine, and all of them let bikers avoid the noise and smell of motor vehicles. Cars and RVs are not admitted at these campsites.

Best of all, hiker/biker campsites are evening gathering places where bikers meet, swap stories and compare body aches.

Oregon Coastal Weather Monthly Averages				
	Jan-Mar	Apr-Jun	Jul-Sep	Oct-Dec
Temperature (F)	45	53	59	50
Precipitation (inches)	11.9	3.6	1.4	10
Days of measurable rain	19	13	7	17
Wind direction	SW	W	NW	SW

Can there be any clearer argument than the chart above? Bike the coast in July through September, and bike it north to south. Since less than five percent of the Oregon coast's famous rain falls in July, August and September, these three months are a biker's window of opportunity. The air is always clean at the coast, and daytime summer temperatures are usually in the 60s and 70s, seldom hot, never muggy. The shoulder months of June and October can also hold nice weather for weeks at a time, but you're pushing your luck. The weather in those months can turn blustery and miserable, and chances of a drenching increase. Fog can roll in at any time of year on the coast, but it appears most frequently in the mornings and soon burns off. Don't bike in fog.

Wind is the big reason to bike from north to south. During July, August and September, the northerlies will be experienced as fresh summer breezes, pushing a loaded bike south. Bikers coming the other way — with their shoulders hunched and the wind whistling across their handle bars — have a much tougher time of it.

Equipment

All kinds of bikes run the coastal route, from sleek road bikes to stumpy mountain bikes. The experts at bike shops along the way vary their recommendations but are unanimous in their loathing for the very expensive, custom-built, odd tire-sized, exotic machines that are hard to repair. Ten speeds are more than enough. The bike route is on hard-surface shoulder all the way, so tires need not be wide. Wide tires should be fully inflated to minimize road resistance. The main thing for any extended trip is that the bike be properly adjusted to the rider's own comfort level. Essential safety equipment includes a helmet, a rear-view mirror and bright clothing. A fluorescent vest or fanny triangle helps make a biker visible to traffic, and visibility is especially important on the coastal route.

Getting to Astoria

The nearest major airport is Portland International, 102 miles from Astoria up the Columbia River.

The Beach Bus, (503) 232-1741, runs once a day from Portland to Tillamook and Seaside. Catch it at Portland's Greyhound Station, which is about eight miles of city biking from the airport. From Seaside, the North Coast Transit Bus, (503) 738-7083, goes to Astoria. These buses have racks to carry unboxed bicycles.

The most common way to start a bike trip from Astoria is to carry the bike there on the rack of a car. Check in at the Visitor Information Center, 111 W. Marine Drive, for long-term parking.

To bike from Portland to Astoria, U.S. Highway 30 is the best route. The road has an ample shoulder and offers occasional views of the Columbia River. A pair of tough thirty-minute climbs — one out of Rainier, the other out of Westport — make it more than most baggage-laden bikers will want to tackle in one day. Summer winds, if any, will be in your face. Rainier and Clatskanie have budget motels, nothing fancy, and no public campgrounds. Arrival by bicycle from the north is easy and safe. Avoid Washington's Route 4, from Longview to the Astoria Bridge. Otherwise, Washington access roads to the Astoria Bridge are either lightly traveled or well shouldered.

CREDITS

Cover design: Elizabeth Watson

Cover photo: Nancy Botta

Author's picture: Pam Casciate

Maps: Debbie Emory

About the maps: Since bikers often remove maps and place them in a handle-bar map case. The maps in this book have been located so they can be removed without losing any of the text.

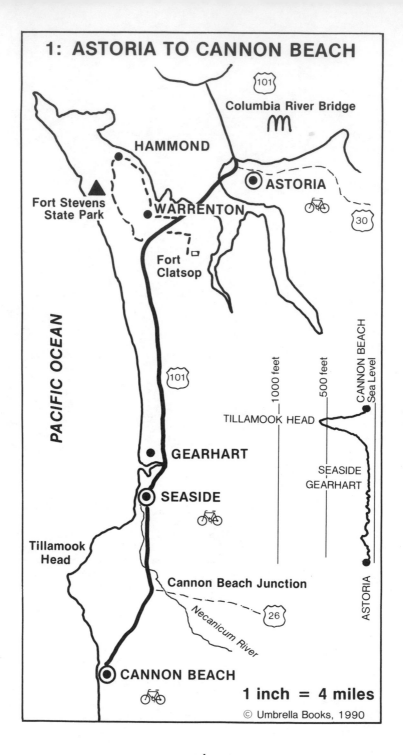

1: ASTORIA TO CANNON BEACH

101

Columbia River Bridge

HAMMOND

ASTORIA

Fort Stevens
State Park

WARRENTON

30

Fort
Clatsop

PACIFIC OCEAN

101

1000 feet

500 feet

CANNON BEACH
Sea Level

TILLAMOOK HEAD

GEARHART

SEASIDE
GEARHART

SEASIDE

Tillamook
Head

ASTORIA

Cannon Beach Junction

26

Necanicum River

CANNON BEACH

1 inch = 4 miles

© Umbrella Books, 1990

xvi

Chapter 1

ASTORIA TO CANNON BEACH

(23 Miles)

The first leg of the Oregon Coast bike trip is an easy one, short and flat. It's a chance to shake the kinks out and get used to the bicycle.

From Astoria to Seaside, U.S. Highway 101 has no hills at all. The road follows a trough between dunes on the right and Coast Range on the left. Dunes hide the surf from view, but the ocean can be reached on practically any road that turns right off Highway 101. After Seaside, the route follows the relaxed Necanicum River inland for about four miles and then offers the day's only mandatory ascent. A gradual climb over the back shoulder of Tillamook Head reaches an elevation of 350 feet. Then comes the glide back to sea level and Cannon Beach.

This chapter's places of historical interest are bunched at the start — in and around Astoria. Just across the Youngs Bay Bridge from Astoria are Fort Stevens and Fort Clatsop. Exploring one or both of these by bike is a good way to make the trip longer and more interesting.

ASTORIA

First things first. Astoria was the first permanent American settlement west of the Mississippi. Here at the junction of the Columbia River and the Pacific Ocean was the first U.S. post office west of the Rockies. Astoria lies within view of the place where Lewis and Clark first spied the Pacific Ocean, in November 1805.

The Euro-American presence here began in 1811 as Fort Astor, a remote outpost of John Jacob Astor's Pacific Fur Company. Hurrying to capitalize on the discoveries of Lewis and Clark, the Americans established a trading post ahead of the Russians, Spanish and British, all of whom had territorial designs on the Oregon Country. An excellent book about this period is *Astoria*, written in 1836 by Washington Irving. Irving and J.J. Astor were friends. Astor himself never set foot on the ground that bears his name, but he fired Irving's imagination and helped give us a detailed and entertaining account of how the fur trade shaped the culture of this place.

The early abundance of fur brought trading ships. Trappers, Indians and tradesmen came down the river to meet them. When fur-bearing native species began to play out, timber and salmon dominated Astorian commerce. Astoria hummed with the sound of sawmills. The smells of fresh-cut lumber and fish canneries filled the moist air, and the hurdy-gurdies in Astoria's dance halls and gaming rooms played to the largest crowds north of San Francisco.

Timber and salmon, in turn, became depleted. Astoria, once Oregon's second-largest city, found itself at the mouth of a river that had changed from a commercial highway to a commercial barrier. The advent of railroads and automobiles returned Astoria to the condition of its birth and youth: an outpost.

Like an old gambler down on his luck, Astoria is richer in memories than in current wealth. Today huge freighters and tankers bypass Astoria on their way to deepwater ports upstream. Although Astoria is smaller and less prominent than it was, it clings to its proud history. Scandinavians, and especially Finns, dominated boomtown Astoria at the turn of the century. Today a quick glance at the Astoria phone book finds Niemi, Nikkila, Nordstrom, Norgaard — Scandinavian names whose ancestors settled here and stuck.

Biking Astoria itself is not easy, because the town is mostly vertical, clinging to steep a hillside. For a quick tour of Astoria's fine Victorian residences and historical buildings, however, pedal east on Franklin from Eleventh to Seventeenth Streets. Then ride or push the bike one block up to Grand, and return to Fourteenth. Along this fairly horizontal loop lie four of Astoria's bed and breakfast places and many other baronial homes that date from more opulent times.

Flavel House

A sensational, almost terrifying, example of Queen Anne architecture is the Flavel House. The grounds of this stern and flamboyant monster occupy an entire city block between Seventh and Eighth, Duane and Exchange Streets.

George Flavel, a native of New Jersey, came to the North Pacific by way of the California goldfields in 1849. Flavel was a twenty-seven-year-old ship's mate when the Oregon territorial government awarded him the first pilot's license to guide marine traffic across the Columbia River bar. With an adept sense of treacherous waters and a shrewd sense of commerce, Captain Flavel held a virtual monopoly over the bar pilotage for more than thirty years. He also ran a tug and wharf business. By the time he retired, in 1887, Flavel was said to be the area's first millionaire.

Flavel built this mansion in 1885. It has been renovated, but never significantly altered. Deeded to Clatsop County for public benefit in 1933, the home served as headquarters for the Red Cross during World War II.

Jail

Easier than Flavel House to comprehend is the Clatsop County Jail, a structure with a clear and unmistakable purpose. Squatting directly across Duane Street from Flavel House, this building was one of the longest continuously-operated (1914 to 1976) jails in the West. The Clatsop County Historical Society is negotiating to buy the jail from the county and to use it as a museum.

The Waldorf

Astor, an American immigrant, was born in the German village of Waldorf. At 1067 Duane Street, Astoria has its Waldorf Hotel. One of Astoria's oldest buildings, the Waldorf-in-Astoria is undergoing renovation for its resumed use as a hotel.

3

Fort Astor

A small historical park at the corner of Fifteenth and Exchange Streets marks the original site of Astoria. In 1811, Astor's men made a clearing in the forest and erected a crude log shelter. When news of the War of 1812 reached Fort Astor in 1813, the Americans were expecting a long-overdue supply ship from Astor's New York headquarters. In a precipitous move that bordered on panic, the Americans abandoned their infant trading post. England's aggressive North West Fur Company moved in and renamed it Fort George.

Not until 1846 did the U.S. and British settle their old border dispute and divide Oregon Country at the 49th Parallel, the present U.S.-Canadian boundary. Oregon was organized in 1848 as a territory, including the land of present-day Washington and Idaho. What we now think of as Oregon became a state of the American Union just yesterday, in 1859.

Heritage Center Museum

This neo-classical building at Sixteenth and Duane Streets was City Hall from the time it was built, in 1905, until Astoria's commercial center gravitated block-by-block westward and away from it. The city's governors moved. The building stayed. It served as the USO during World War II and as the Maritime Museum in the 1960s and 1970s.

The Waterfront

On the river between Ninth and Eleventh Streets are delis, gift shops, art galleries and restaurants. Park the bike and walk. Rough-cut planks on the piers have gaps wide enough to swallow a bicycle wheel to the hub. As sunset nears, a good place to be is the Feed Store Restaurant or Lounge, on Pier 11. From here there is a fine view of ship and fishing boat traffic. Commercial fishing boats unload at the nearby dock, and seals or sea lions often cavort and celebrate around this activity.

Visitors should be aware that it is a major gaffe in Astoria to admire seals and sea lions. These voracious sea-going mammals follow salmon and steelhead into the Columbia estuary and come into direct

4

ecological conflict with those other sea-going mammals, the Astoria fishermen. The prevailing view here is that the best use of a seal is for a fur coat. Any visitor who cannot bring himself to embrace this view will do just as well to keep his mouth shut.

Columbia River Maritime Museum

At the foot of Seventeenth Street in Astoria is the Northwest's best maritime museum. Here in the ship-wreck gallery is ample evidence to support the Columbia River bar's reputation as "The Graveyard of the Pacific." Over 2,000 craft, including 200 major vessels, have succumbed to storm, hazardous currents or plain bad judgment on the perilous waters of the bar.

Museum visitors can stand their turn at the wheel of a turn-of-the-century river steamer, or train a periscope on the Washington shore, four miles distant. The evolution of fishing methods is well-documented, and there are restored gillnet boats and Coast Guard lifeboats.

The last *Columbia River Lightship*, which marked the river entrance from 1951 to 1980, is docked next to the museum and is open to visitors. The Coast Guard has replaced this lightship with an unmanned and fully automated navigational buoy.

The View from Astoria Column

On the theory that it can be immensely satisfying – a confidence builder – to start this bicycle trip with a climb that is steeper than anything else on the entire coastal route, we recommend a jaunt up the hill to the Astoria Column.

A memorial to the westward sweep of discovery and migration, the column is 1.4 miles from the Maritime Museum. It sits atop Coxcomb Hill, at an elevation of 595 feet. A fading frieze of frontier history spirals up the column's sides, and the interior staircase rises to one of the West's most exhilarating panoramic views.

Below lies the Columbia River, pushing out to sea. The river's drainage starts at the Continental Divide and covers most of Oregon, Washington, Idaho and western Montana. It also drains parts of

Wyoming and a good share of British Columbia. The Columbia's water volume is ten times the flow of the Colorado River, double the volume of the Missouri River.

The outlet of this "Great River of the West" baffled the coast's early explorers. The Spanish captain Bruno de Hezeta took a look as he passed along the Pacific Coast in 1775. Hezeta suspected a great river here, but his crew was too reduced by illness and death for him to investigate. A year later the English captain James Cook passed the mouth of the Columbia without recognizing it. In 1788, John Meares, an independent trader, arrived at the location of Hezeta's reported river. Not finding it, Meares named the low promontory that guards the river mouth: Cape Disappointment.

From atop the Astoria Column, sight over the right peak of the highest point on the Astoria Bridge. The tiny white dot on the distant shore is Cape Disappointment Lighthouse. The cape is home to the U.S. Coast Guard station with the highest rate of emergency rescue missions. This is where the Coast Guard trains its search and rescue boat operators.

At about one o'clock from Cape Disappointment is the section of the river's far (Washington) shore where the great one-eyed Chinook Indian Chief, Concomly, had his main village. Concomly and his tribe traded eagerly with early white sailors and guided them in the ways of the river. The Indians' hospitality was repaid, however, by a white man's land claim to the freshwater springs that fed the Chinook village. Natives who had not already succumbed to smallpox were forced off the land.

Just to the right of where the bridge meets the rocky Washington shore, the Lewis and Clark party was pinned by storm and fierce water in November of 1805. For five days they were unable to retreat or advance. Punished by rain, wind and cold, hampered by low visibility, they confused the saltwater taste of the wide river for the Pacific itself. Clark wrote in his journal of having arrived at the ocean long before, in fact, he did.

The wide inlet at about three o'clock on the far shore is Gray's Bay. The American trader Robert Gray, after sailing around Cape

6

Horn from Boston, anchored the *Columbia Rediviva* here in 1792. His was the first white party to cross the bar. On behalf of the United States, he claimed the entire drainage of the river and named it after his ship.

This harbor was as far up the river as the thirty-seven-year-old Gray ever navigated. The fact that Gray didn't sail beyond the reach of saltwater became a bone of contention for the British, who sailed upriver to the site of present-day Portland a year later. William Broughton, a lieutenant of George Vancouver, spied and named Mt. Hood. He claimed the entire river drainage for the Crown. The question was: Had Gray, before Broughton, entered the *river*? Or had Gray simply explored an extension of *the ocean*, as Eighteenth Century maritime law defined any body of water within the reach of saltwater?

If not for the border settlement of 1846, Americans today might be carrying passports to this spot. Visitors would pay in pounds and shillings for Astoria's fish and chips.

When you're ready to put Astoria in the rear-view mirror and head south, pick up Highway 101 where it comes off the Astoria Bridge and meets Marine Drive. This guide will note mileage as if bikers never left the main route north-to-south, not because we don't recommend side trips and poking around, but because it provides an easy reference.

Mile

0.0   Astoria, at Marine Drive and the bridge. Take Highway 101 South. The bridge across the Columbia was completed in 1966. Before then, the only way for a car to cross the river within fifty miles of Astoria was by ferry.

0.6   The low Youngs Bay Bridge has minimal shoulder for one mile. Be alert.

2.7   Youngs Bay Plaza. The road to the right leads to Warrenton, Hammond and Fort Stevens, a good side trip. (See page 8.)

3.3   The turnoff, left, to Alternate 101 and Fort Clatsop, another terrific side trip. (See pages 9-10.)

Side Trip: Fort Stevens

From Highway 101 at Youngs Bay Plaza, follow signs seaward through the small fishing ports of Warrenton and Hammond to Fort Stevens. The historical area and museum are 4.8 miles from Highway 101, along perfectly flat road.

The Union built Fort Stevens during the Civil War, girding itself against the possibility of Confederate frigates mounting a far western offensive. That threat never materialized, but from 1897 to 1904 came a massive military build-up, including the construction of eight huge, concrete gun batteries.

Easily the most famous day in the history of Fort Stevens was Sunday, June 21, 1942. Shortly before midnight, a Japanese submarine I-25 fired seventeen concussion rounds at Fort Stevens. They didn't hit anything, but the shots blasted wide depressions in the sand and exploded onto the next morning's eight-column headline in *The San Francisco News*: OREGON COAST SHELLED!

In the annals of warfare, it wasn't much. The Army didn't fire back. But Fort Stevens is the only military installation in the forty-eight contiguous states to have been fired upon since the War of 1812.

When Fort Stevens artillerymen were not allowed to fire back, they were so disgusted that a reported twenty-two of them went AWOL. Their superiors later explained the lack of retaliation by saying that the sub was out of range (unlikely), or that returning fire would have given away the guns' exact location. One report says the officer who had the key to the armory couldn't be found. Another report dismisses the whole fiasco with the observation that hitting a sub at sea would have been about as likely as a golfer making a hole in one.

From the museum and historical area, eight miles of off-road bike path lead to the attractions of Fort Stevens State Park:

- A viewing platform at the junction of Pacific Surf and South Jetty;

- The wreck of the *Peter Iredale*, a four-masted grain barque from Liverpool. Her navigators, in 1906, misjudged their approach to the bar and beached her on flat sands, where her remains sit rusting today;

- Coffenbury Lake, a nice place for a swim;

- The campground, a verdant, wind-protected place always crowded with biking families in July and August.

Another Side Trip: Fort Clatsop

Just half a mile past the junction of Highway 101 and Youngs Bay Plaza, take a left. Brown signs mark the 3.3-mile trip to Fort Clatsop National Memorial. This is where the Lewis and Clark party spent its miserable winter of 1805-06. From December 7 to March 23, they experienced only six days without rain.

Had there been an Oregon Tourist Bureau, the Lewis and Clark party might have been induced to stay the summer at this mild and beautiful spot. As it was, they returned overland to beat the 1806 winter across the Rockies and report their discoveries to an eager nation.

The National Park Service reconstructed the fort from Clark's sketch of the floor plan. The wonder is how such a tiny structure could have housed a party of thirty men, plus Sacajawea and her baby. The Lewis and Clark party chose this site for its natural shelter from wind, its freshwater springs, and its proximity to deer and elk. Still, the explorers had to endure the cold, the damp and the fleas that the friendly and otherwise helpful Clatsop Indians shared with their visitors.

> Summer activities at Fort Clatsop include a living history program. Actors in buckskin make candles, shoot muzzle-loading flintlocks and launch pirogues. At the visitor center, Lorne Green narrates a twenty-seven-minute film about Lewis and Clark and the Corps of Discovery.

Mile

5.7   The south exit road from Fort Stevens State Park rejoins Highway 101.

6.1   Turnoff to Camp Rilea, which is now used for training by the Oregon National Guard, and to the Pioneer Cemetery.

7.3   Astoria Country Club, on the right. Golfers on these green dunes have never known a flat lie.

11.4   Turnoff to Del Rey Beach Wayside.

13.1   The stop light at Gearhart. It's not Carmel-by-the-Sea, but Gearhart has long been popular with wealthy and socially prominent Oregonians. Residents have managed to resist the more garish forms of seaside commercial development. Turn right for a quick loop to the beach and a look at this quiet, tasteful place.

13.9   Entering Seaside. After crossing the Necanicum River bridge, follow signs to City Center.

15.5   The traffic light at Holladay and Broadway.

Seaside

The closest beach town to Portland, Seaside gathers a lot of day trippers and weekend cruisers. Broadway, toward the beach, is the main drag. The smell is of caramel corn, saltwater taffy and corn dogs. Pinball machines and shooting galleries are noisier than the sea gulls until the turnaround, at the end of Broadway.

From the turnaround, which the Oregon Legislature designated "the end of the Lewis and Clark Trail," a two-mile promenade lines the beach front and is open to slow bicycle traffic.

The site of Lewis and Clark's Salt Works is eight blocks south of the turnaround and one block inland, at South Beach Drive and Lewis & Clark Way. Here the Corps of Discovery boiled seawater to make about three quarts of salt a day for seasoning and preservative. They couldn't do it closer to Fort Clatsop because the influence of the Columbia River made seawater there insufficiently saline.

Mile

16.0   Holladay Drive rejoins Highway 101.

18.7   Cannon Beach Junction. Stay on Highway 101 South, and start the climb.

21.6   Viewpoint and historical marker. William Clark brought a hungry crew to Ecola Creek in January 1806 to investigate rumors of a beached whale. They found the 105-foot whale skeleton and bought oil and blubber from the local Indians who had stripped it.

22.5   Turn right off Highway 101 for Cannon Beach.

22.8   The turnoff to Ecola State Park. It is a beautiful but strenuous side trip, up and down through virgin stands of spruce, hemlock and Douglas fir. The first viewpoint and picnic spot is above Crescent Beach, three miles in. Here are spectacular views of Cannon Beach and Haystack Rock, to the south. The offshore islands are a resting spot for sea lions and shore birds. A steep path, impassable to bikes, leads to the beach.

23.3   Downtown Cannon Beach.

Cannon Beach

Cannon Beach is an upscale resort that arranges itself like an audience around Haystack Rock, probably the most photographed monolith on the Oregon Coast.

With good luck or careful advance planning, a visitor might arrive for the Sand Castle Sculpture Contest in early summer. At any time of year, the Cannon Beach sky is apt to be filled with bizarre and colorful kites. The seven-mile beach will be spotted with joggers, beachcombers, horseback riders and evening campfire worshipers.

The Coaster Theater in Cannon Beach offers year-round live theater, concerts, comedy and musical revues. Cannon Beach also teems with art, pottery and sculpture galleries. Cute boutiques — with names like Once Upon a Breeze, Thistledown Gifts, Sometimes a Great Lotion — are the hallmark of Cannon Beach.

But the ice cream is good after a day of biking.

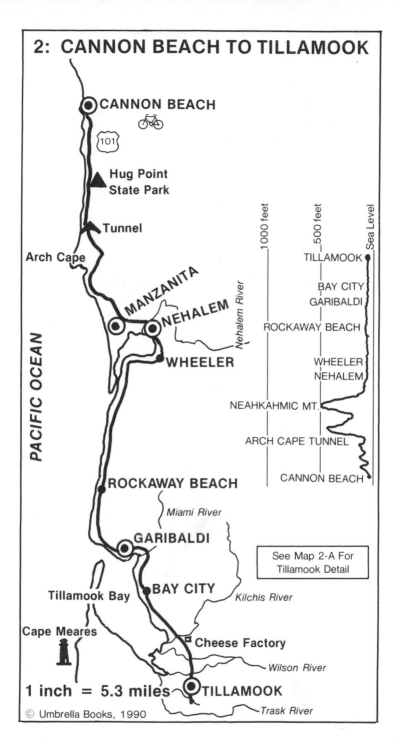

2: CANNON BEACH TO TILLAMOOK

CANNON BEACH

101

Hug Point
State Park

Tunnel

Arch Cape

PACIFIC OCEAN

MANZANITA

NEHALEM

Nehalem River

WHEELER

ROCKAWAY BEACH

Miami River

GARIBALDI

Tillamook Bay

BAY CITY

Kilchis River

Cape Meares

Cheese Factory

Wilson River

1 inch = 5.3 miles

TILLAMOOK

Trask River

© Umbrella Books, 1990

1000 feet

500 feet

Sea Level

TILLAMOOK

BAY CITY
GARIBALDI

ROCKAWAY BEACH

WHEELER
NEHALEM

NEAHKAHMIC MT.

ARCH CAPE TUNNEL

CANNON BEACH

See Map 2-A For
Tillamook Detail

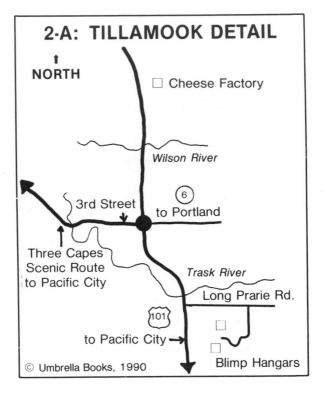

2-A: TILLAMOOK DETAIL

↑
NORTH

☐ Cheese Factory

Wilson River

③rd Street

⑥ to Portland

Three Capes
Scenic Route
to Pacific City

Trask River

Long Prarie Rd.

(101)

to Pacific City →

© Umbrella Books, 1990

☐
☐
Blimp Hangars

Chapter 2

CANNON BEACH TO TILLAMOOK

(41 Miles)

This leg of the trip starts with pleasing views of Cannon Beach and its rocky coastline as Hemlock Street dips and winds out of town. Later, when the road cuts to the seaward side of Neahkahnie (Nee-ah-KAW-nee) Mountain, bikers get a higher and more breathtaking look at the ocean below. From Manzanita to Tillamook—the final two-thirds of this leg—the route is flat and easy. Highway 101 follows the Nehalem River for a while. Then it parallels the long, straight sands toward Rockaway Beach. Finally the road bends onto the wide, historic and fish-rich Tillamook Bay.

The day's principal climb is a double-barrel affair, like the humps on a camel, around Cape Falcon and Neahkahnie Mountain. The scariest part is the tunnel, one of two on the Oregon coastal route. Follow the safety instructions at the tunnel and pedal hard.

Mile

0.0   Cannon Beach, at Hemlock and First Streets. Take Hemlock Street south until it dead-ends at Highway 101.

2.6   Rejoin Highway 101 South.

3.9   Hug Point State Park. Hiker/biker campground.

5.5   Historical marker about the naming of Cannon Beach. In 1846 the *Shark*, a U.S. Navy schooner on a surveying mission, grounded on a spit as she crossed the Columbia River Bar. In a futile effort to free the *Shark,* the crew chopped down her masts and jettisoned the cannons. Part of her deck, with a small iron cannon attached to it, drifted ashore near this spot. The cannon, after suffering from exposure and vandalism at this site next to Highway 101, was moved in 1989 to Astoria's Heritage Museum.

6.9   Arch Cape Tunnel. For a tunnel, it's well-lit. And from the start, the end of the tunnel is visible. The roadway through the tunnel does have a narrow shoulder, but....

CAUTION: Pull off the road before the tunnel entrance. When ready to go, push the button to activate yellow flashing lights that warn traffic of bikes in the tunnel. As an added precaution, wait until there is no oncoming traffic in sight before pushing the button and entering the tunnel.

7.1   The tunnel exit marks the start of a 1.7-mile climb.

10.5   Oswald West State Park. Park the bike and walk toward the ocean for a hundred yards or so for a look at one of the most pristine and spectacular sections of Oregon coast.

Oregonians, and everybody who bikes or visits this coast, can thank ex-governor Oswald "Os" West and the 1913 state legislature for giving the state title to over four hundred miles of Oregon beaches. West, the governor from 1911 to 1945, was a tireless defender of the idea, as he put it, that "Beaches should remain as God made them." In his first term of office, West championed legislation that declared the seashore a state highway. Individuals or private entities could own property overlooking the beach, but the beach itself became a public heritage. In the sweeping 1969 court case of *Thorndike* v. *Hay,* the Oregon Supreme Court further defined West's notion by declaring that all Oregon beaches — between mean high tide and the visible line of vegetation — must be accessible for public recreation and enjoyment.

On the subject of good laws, here we might note that Oregon's "Bottle Law," which calls for a nickel deposit on cans and bottles, helps keep the roadside relatively free of debris and broken glass.

From Oswald West State Park, there's a 1.8-mile ascent to Highway 101's summit on Neahkahnie Mountain.

Mile

11.7   Viewpoint. Oswald West hired a state highway engineer, Samuel H. Boardman, who is largely responsible for the beautiful rockwork (1930s) that lines the coast highway next to oceanside cliffs. More about Boardman, who became superintendent of state parks, later.

12.3   Neahkahnie Summit. Viewpoint. Indian stories include a variety of references to Neahkahnie as a chief deity who turned to stone. Early inhabitants were fascinated with, and terrified of, the place. This headland has been a place of mystery and intrigue through more recent written history, as well. Survivors of a wrecked Spanish galleon are said to have buried their treasure chests at the foot of Neahkahnie Mounain. Efforts to locate that treasure have been feverish, sometimes sophisticated and always — to date — futile.

Tucked below the rocky headland of Neahkahnie is the village of Manzanita. Just beyond that is Nehalem Bay. Tillamook Bay hides behind the jetty in the far distance. Other bikers are grinning not just because of the view but also because the route is all downhill from here.

14.4   Manzanita Junction. The town, a quiet and traditional enclave of summer homes, hides from Highway 101 near the ocean. Golf course, delis.

15.1   Turn off to Nehalem Bay State Park. The hiker/biker campground is two miles from Highway 101.

16.2   Nehalem (Neh-HAY-lum). Arts and crafts galleries abound, and the rustic mall boasts fifty antique dealers under one roof.

In the fall, Nehalem's attention turns to Chinook runs in the nearby river of the same name.

18.6   Wheeler. E.E. Lytle brought the railroad line to town in 1911, and Wheeler became the site of many canneries and lumber mills. When those industries declined, the train tracks fell into disuse. In 1989, however, the newly-formed Oregon Coastline Express put an engine and two cheery passenger cars on the tracks to carry sightseers between Tillamook and Wheeler. The train runs two round trips a day, three on weekends. Tickets are for sale at the stations in Wheeler, Rockaway Beach, Garibaldi and Tillamook.

24.7   Rockaway Beach. If a coastal town could ever be described as featureless, this is the one. The beach stretches for miles, flat and wide, a great place for flying colorful kites. To bypass the traffic on Highway 101 for a while, jog right at Nineteenth Avenue and take Miller Street south. Turn oceanward again at Eleventh Avenue and follow Pacific Street as far as it goes before rejoining Highway 101.

29.3   Barview Store. Turn right and bike 150 yards for a view of the jetty and Tillamook Bay's bar.

30.0   First full view of Tillamook Bay. Early seafarers thought this expanse might be the outlet of the "Great River of the West." In fact the bay's source is smaller streams—the Miami, the Kilchis, the Wilson, and the Trask—which are best suited for canoes and other small boats.

31.0   Garibaldi, Seventh Street. Wharf access (described below).

Garibaldi

One of the first white settlers in the Tillamook Bay area named this community after the Italian revolutionary figure. Today Garibaldi is best known for its commercial and sport fishing.

Turn bayward at Seventh Street to loop the wharves. Charter boats, depending on the season, take visitors salmon fishing, deep-sea bottom fishing or crabbing. At the docks, the charter boat firms will vacuum-pack and mail away your catch, thereby circumventing the clumsy and smelly business of transporting fish or crabs by bicycle.

For non-fishermen, there are excursions of one to five hours to watch whales or just to putter around Tillamook Bay. The area looks very different from the water.

Mile

33.5   Historical Marker. Captain Robert Gray, sailing from Boston in the sloop *Lady Washington,* rode favorable wind and tide conditions over the Tillamook bar on August 14, 1788. Gray was in search of furs to sell in China. He anchored in the bay near this spot and flew the American flag for the first time in Oregon country.

Natives of a nearby village, probably at Garibaldi, were friendly. In exchange for trivial gifts, they brought crabs, fish and much-needed berries and fruit to the ship. As a party of sailors went ashore to gather grass for the animals on board, however, trouble broke out. According to the account of Second Mate Robert Haswell, one of the natives seized a cutlass belonging to Marcus Lopius, a young African crewman. The Indian took off, and Lopius chased him. A fight ensued, in which Indians speared Lopius to death and the Boston men fired a lot of shots. Lopius's body was left on the beach while the others scrambled, unharmed, to the relative safety of the ship and its cannons. It is unclear how many, if any, Indians died in this skirmish.

In any event, the tide of hospitality had turned. The natives howled and circled menacingly in canoes. They lit mean bonfires at night. Gray tried to leave, but summer winds made it much harder to sail out of the bay than it had been to sail into it. Not until August 18, in his third day of trying to buck the wind, was Gray able to leave what he called Murderer's Harbor. Four years later — on a different trip, in a different ship — Gray sailed into and named the Columbia River.

19

Mile

35.5 Bay City, a small town with groceries and fishing tackle, to the left of the highway.

38.3 Cross the Kilchis River. Kilchis, a Tillamook chief during the pioneer period, was widely respected for his wisdom and his physical stature. Historians have beat themselves to a froth trying to account for the fact that early white settlers described Kilchis as having had such non-Indian features as a curly beard, kinky hair, a flat nose and fat lips. Perhaps an ancestor of Kilchis survived the wreck of a Spanish galleon that plied this coast. Africans often sailed on those ships. One theory is that Gray's African crewman, Marcus Lopius, wasn't killed after all and fathered Kilchis by a native wife. Nobody knows. Maybe the early Europeans' obsession with race led them to exaggerate Kilchis' features and build him into this Othello-like being. By all accounts, however, Kilchis was a big man, a great chief.

39.2 Tillamook Cheese Factory (described below). Visitor Information Center.

41.1 Tillamook. Junction of Highways 101 and 6.

TILLAMOOK

The name comes from local Indians who appear in early written accounts as the Callemeux, the Killamox or the Killamuch. Tillamook finally took hold. The word means "Land of many waters."

The town's first white settler was the strange and taciturn Joseph Champion, whose notoriety spread among Indians as "the man who lived in a tree." Champion arrived in 1851 and set up housekeeping in the hollowed-out trunk of a Sitka spruce. Word of this odd pioneer in a bounteous land soon reached the Willamette Valley, and the curious white settlers who followed Champion to Tillamook Bay were mostly farmers.

Tillamook was a jewel of a place for farming, especially dairy farming. Between the steep rise of the coastal mountains and the wide waters of Tillamook Bay lie lush, green, sponge-like fields where milk cows thrived. The trouble was — has always been — access to markets. The bar was a barrier to sea traffic, and the trip over the Coast Range to the Willamette Valley was not only arduous but time-consuming. Milk would spoil before the farmers could get it to market. That's why the dairy farmers became cheesemakers.

In a word-association test these days, "Tillamook" and "cheese" are still natural partners. The virgin forests have been scalped and the fishing isn't what it used to be, but the grass keeps coming. These Holstein cattle grazing in the fields make rich, sweet milk which supplies the local cheese plant. Tillamook High School teams compete as The Cheesemakers.

Within Oregon, Tillamook's fame is tied as closely to fish as to cheese. Tillamook Bay and its tributaries are home to the big ones, fall Chinook salmon. From September to December, they enter the bay from the Pacific Ocean and make their way upstream to spawn. Until the mid-1980s, Chinook salmon runs were in steady decline. Recent treaties between Canada and the U.S., along with stricter catch limits, shorter fishing seasons and better hatcheries, appear to be restoring the runs. A fifty-pound salmon is no longer newsworthy, as it would have been ten years ago, but a sixty pounder is unusual. In 1987, fishing guide Bob Tolman's boat landed a seventy-pound Chinook in upper Tillamook Bay.

Tillamook Cheese Factory

The famous factory is two miles north of Tillamook center, on Highway 101. T.F. Townsend built the area's first cheese factory in 1894, and by 1909 there were ten of them in Tillamook. The Tillamook County Creamery Association, a cooperative, was formed to control quality and to coordinate marketing. When the cooperative's cheddar took first prize at the 1914 St. Louis World's Fair, the reputation of Tillamook Cheese spread beyond the West. Today the factory turns out thirty million pounds of world-renowned cheddars each year. Visitors are welcome. Watch the cheese-making process from milk to curds and whey, to cheddaring and chopping into forty-pound blocks. Their ice cream, too, is good.

21

On the factory grounds is a replica of *Morning Star*, a tiny ship that in the very early days was the only way of getting dairy products out of Tillamook. Local farmers were cut off from the navigable world when the captain of their supply and delivery ship died, and nobody else would cross the bar to serve them. So they banded together to build the *Morning Star* themselves. A very good, short historical novel about this episode is Don Berry's *To Build a Ship*. One of the characters in this book is the enigmatic Joseph Champion, who lived in a tree.

Tillamook County Pioneer Museum

The grand building at Pacific Avenue and First Street was once the Tillamook County Court House. It was built in 1905 and became a museum in 1935. On the second floor is one of the state's best natural history exhibits. Other highlights include a replica of Joe Champion's tree-house, a cannon ball that is thought to have been fired ashore during Gray's fight with the Indians, and a display about the Tillamook Naval Air Station's blimp hangars. Learn here, also, about the devastating 1933 Tillamook Burn, which wiped out 240,000 acres of prime forest between here and the Willamette Valley.

Blimp Hangars

The two largest free-standing wooden structures in the world rise from the flat pastures near Tillamook. To get there, bike 2.5 miles south from Tillamook center on Highway 101. Turn left on Long Prairie Road for another mile. When they say, "You can't miss it," that's not a cliche. Seven football games could be played simultaneously in each of these buildings, and they are 195 feet tall.

Left over from World War II, these monsters housed the blimps of the U.S. Naval Lighter-Than-Air Station. Navy blimps escorted warships and patrolled the coast for enemy submarines. Today, one hangar is used to refurbish railroad cars. The other still houses blimps. AeroLift's CycloCrane, for example, is used for logging, for ferrying material to inaccessible construction sites and for rescue missions. There are advertising blimps, surveillance blimps. The active blimp hangar isn't officially open to the public, but they have to keep the door open for ventilation, and it's hard to hide a blimp. Anybody can sneak a peek at these amazing machines, indoors.

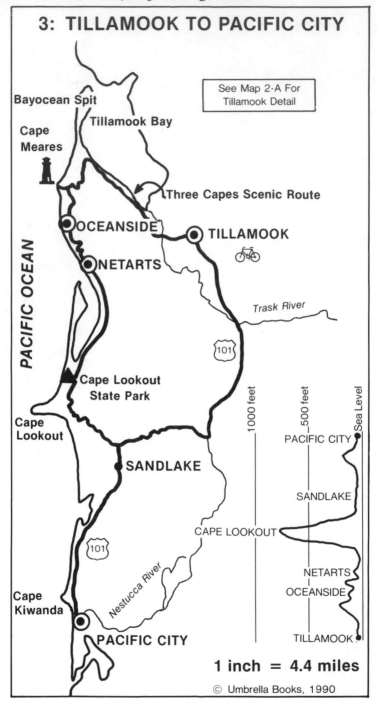

3: TILLAMOOK TO PACIFIC CITY

See Map 2-A For
Tillamook Detail

Bayocean Spit

Tillamook Bay

Cape
Meares

Three Capes Scenic Route

PACIFIC OCEAN

OCEANSIDE

TILLAMOOK

NETARTS

Trask River

101

Cape Lookout
State Park

Cape
Lookout

1000 feet

500 feet

Sea Level

PACIFIC CITY

SANDLAKE

SANDLAKE

101

CAPE LOOKOUT

Nestucca River

NETARTS

Cape
Kiwanda

OCEANSIDE

PACIFIC CITY

TILLAMOOK

1 inch = 4.4 miles

Chapter 3

TILLAMOOK TO PACIFIC CITY

(37 Miles)

The official Oregon Coast Bike Route splits and presents two options at Tillamook. Bikers can choose between the "easy route" and the "scenic route." Both routes bypass a narrow and dangerous section of Highway 101 between the towns of Beaver and Hebo.

The Easy Route: From Tillamook, continue south on Highway 101 for 14.5 miles. Turn right off Highway 101 at the set of signposts that point toward Sandlake and Cape Kiwanda and Pacific City. DON'T MISS THIS TURNOFF: Beyond this point, Highway 101 becomes dangerous for bike traffic. Pedal westward for 4.3 miles to join up with the scenic route at Sandlake Junction, and continue south into Pacific City.

The Scenic Route: From Tillamook, follow the Three Capes Scenic Route all the way to Pacific City. This is the far more interesting branch of the coastal bike route, and it's the branch we choose to describe in detail on the pages that follow. This route, bypassing Highway 101 altogether, is the longer and more difficult option, with a tough climb over Cape Lookout. But the views are terrific, and the traffic is light. The three capes—Meares, Lookout and Kiwanda—offer some of the most varied and thrilling biking on the coast. Along the way there's plenty of flat road, too, giving time to breathe and relax.

Mile

0.0 Tillamook. Junction of Highways 101 and 6. Go west on Third Street and follow signs toward the Three Capes Scenic Route.

1.8 Cross the Trask River. Elbridge Trask was among a group of American explorers, trappers and hunters who sailed around Cape Horn from Boston in 1834 and helped counter the British hold on the Oregon Country. Trask trapped and hunted in the Rocky Mountains for a few years before settling on Clatsop Plains, near present-day Seaside. In 1852, right on the heels of Joseph Champion, Trask moved to Tillamook County. See Don Berry's book, *Trask*, for an account of Trask's dealings with the great Black Indian chief, Kilchis.

1.9 Turn right on Bayocean Road. Follow Tillamook Bay's flat south flank, a favorite haunt of blue herons and egrets. Expect headwinds. For about five miles, the coastal bike route goes northwest. Headed briefly in this "wrong" direction, a biker can appreciate why it was much easier for Robert Gray to sail into Tillamook Bay than to sail out of it.

6.8 Bayocean historical marker. The interesting part is that there is nothing left to see of Bayocean. Bayocean Spit once was the site of a giddy new resort advertised as "The Queen of the Pacific."

In 1906 T.B. Potter, a real estate mogul from Kansas City, envisioned a second Atlantic City on this narrow neck of land between Tillamook Bay and the Pacific Ocean. He formed the Potter-Chapin Realty Co. and went right to work creating a summer resort town on the spit. By 1912, Bayocean had a three-story hotel, a bowling alley and one of Oregon's largest natatoria. The town had paved roads, city lights and a narrow-gauge railway. The lots sold like hotcakes. As in the biblical parable about building on sand, however, Bayocean was doomed to erosion from the sea on one side and the bay on the other. The natatorium crumbled in 1932. Over twenty homes were devoured by the sea. In 1952 the ocean cut a half-mile-wide swath through the peninsula, isolating Bayocean on an island. Of the fifty-nine remaining Bayocean homes and cottages, only five were moved before they fell into the water or were destroyed by waves.

Since 1956, a breakwater has reestablished the spit as a peninsula. Nobody lives there. In the battle between nature and development, chalk one up for nature.

Mile

7.2   Turn left, in the direction of Oceanside, and start the climb. Stop at any of the turnouts toward the top of the hill for a look back at inhospitable Bayocean Spit.

9.1   Turn right to enter Cape Meares State Park. The road to the park winds through magnificent virgin stands of spruce, hemlock and Douglas fir.

10.1   Turnaround at the park.

CAPE MEARES STATE PARK

The cape is named for John Meares, whose retirement from the British Navy was only the beginning of his impact on world affairs. In 1786, the enterprising and off-beat Meares sailed for English merchants from India to Nootka (in present-day British Columbia), where he traded two pistols for a piece of land, erected a small fort and began building his own schooners. Meares was the first to export lumber to China, the first to bring Chinese laborers to this coast and the originator of the trick of sailing under double colors to confuse monopolists and duty collectors.

Having set all this activity in motion, Meares slipped out in the summer of 1788 to do some exploring. His tiny schooner, the *North West America*, passed the mouth of the Columbia on July 6, but Meares didn't recognize it as a river. He sailed on down the coast. On his return past Tillamook Bay, Meares met Robert Gray's ship, the now-famous *Lady Washington*. Meares told Gray he thought Tillamook Bay might be the outlet of their elusive "Great River of the West." Meares didn't try to cross the bar. Gray, as every Oregon schoolchild now knows, did cross the bar.

27

Cape Meares Lighthouse

From the park turnaround, it's less than a minute's walk to Cape Meares Lighthouse, which sits at the crest of a 200-foot cliff over the ocean. The first light, from a five-wick kerosene lantern, was lit in 1890. An eight-sided lens threw white and red beams as a "clockworks" system of gears kept the lens rotating from sunset to sunrise, in all kinds of weather. The lightkeeper's family was so isolated here that most of their food came from their own garden. A teacher came to live with them in winter. The family once wrote of a hair-raising, all-night horse and buggy trip to get to the doctor in Tillamook.

Today, there is no live-in lightkeeper. Since 1963, the Coast Guard blinks an automated light from a blockhouse near the tower.

Octopus Tree

Another short walk from the Cape Meares State Park turn-around is the Octopus Tree. A giant Sitka spruce has matured like a freakish candelabra near the cliffside. Legend has it (probably wrongly) that coastal Indians shaped the tree in its youth to hold their sacred burial canoes. Biologists doubt that such a bizarre living thing could be anything but a work of nature. Coastal weather did it.

Mile

11.1   After exiting the park on the same road you came in on, turn right (south) on the road to Oceanside.

13.6   Oceanside. A collection of old summer cottages and ritzy new vacation homes arranges itself more or less vertically, up the hillside, above a protected seaside cove. Everybody has a view, and it's a good one.

15.9   Netarts (NEE-tarts) Grocery. The prefix *Ne-* is common among north-coast natives who spoke versions of the language called Salishan. In *Necanicum, Neahkahnie, Nehalem, Nestucca, and Neskowin*, the prefix means place, or village, much like the Anglo-Saxon *-ton* and *-burg*. Nobody seems to know what *-tarts* means.

16.3   Turn right on Netarts Bay Drive. Now comes the flat and
        beautiful ride along the estuary of the Netarts River. Three Arch
        Rock soon becomes visible off Cape Meares, to the rear.

18.5   Wee Willie Restaurant is an unlikely-looking place for great
        food. Thick chowder, clam strips, homemade pies and pastries
        are the house specialties.

19.0   Whiskey Creek Fish Hatchery. Tillamook Anglers—a private,
        all-volunteer group—raises spring Chinook to boost Tillamook
        Bay salmon runs. Visitors are welcome.

21.4   Entrance to Cape Lookout State Park. Near the beach in this
        park is the most beautiful, wind-sheltered and secluded
        hiker/biker campground on the coast. Bikers who are not ready
        to camp might consider a nap. The next three miles are all uphill.

        On the way up the hill, stop at each viewpoint for exhilarating
        and probably necessary reminders of why anyone would ride a
        bike up here.

24.2   Road summit, Cape Lookout. Elevation 700 feet. This is as high
        as the Oregon Coast Bike Route ever gets. The descent provides
        spectacular viewpoints toward Cape Kiwanda, Neskowin and
        Cascade Head.

27.5   Sandlake Junction. Turn right (south) toward Sandlake and
        Pacific City. This junction is where the wimps who took the easy
        option from Tillamook rejoin the Three Capes Scenic Route.

28.5   Sandlake Grocery. The road to the right leads to huge sand
        dunes, a lake and a campground that bikers might want to avoid.
        Beer-fueled drivers of dune buggies think this campground is
        heaven. They race all night on summer weekends.

35.4   Dory launch at Cape Kiwanda (described below).

36.6   Pacific City center. Blinking red light.

Cape Kiwanda/Pacific City

Unlike the other two capes the bike route has crossed today, Cape Kiwanda is relatively flat, a welcome change. A low finger of sandstone bluff juts into the ocean and protects the beach to its south from summer winds. Offshore lies another Haystack Rock, like its namesake at Cannon Beach, and the rock helps break the momentum of waves reaching the beach. The surf, therefore, is unusually docile south of Cape Kiwanda. Fishermen can launch their boats directly into the froth instead of having to cross a river bar.

The flat-bottomed, banana-curved fishing boats that get launched directly into the surf are called dories. Their return is the most exciting part. The boats come skidding full-bore onto flat sand like ducks landing on ice. Badly done, it's a disaster. Well done, it's a piece of art.

The annual Pacific City Dory Festival, in mid-July, is when they really show off. Festivities include a boat parade, a fish fry, and dory races through the surf to Haystack Rock.

Men — and increasingly, women — who work the dories may be fishing for sport or for their livelihood. The commercial dories have long wooden poles projecting from the boat. From these poles they drop cannonball-sized weights and can run up to two dozen leaders at a time with plugs, flashers or herring-baited hooks. In July and August they hope to catch the lordly Chinook, but they mostly catch silvers (Coho), a smaller and more plentiful breed of salmon.

With a hot Chinook bite, a commercial dory fishermen can make $500 a day. More common is a day in which he or she weighs in with less than enough fish-flesh to pay for gas. For fish stories, go to Sportsmen's Tavern, near Pacific City's lone stoplight. For the truth, watch them unload and weigh in at the seafood company, right across the street from where the dories beach: "We fished all *@#*ing morning and killed two *@#*ing silvers," says Belinda the fisherman, pocketing $10.82 for her and her partner's day's work. "*@#* it."

Life is hard in the West.

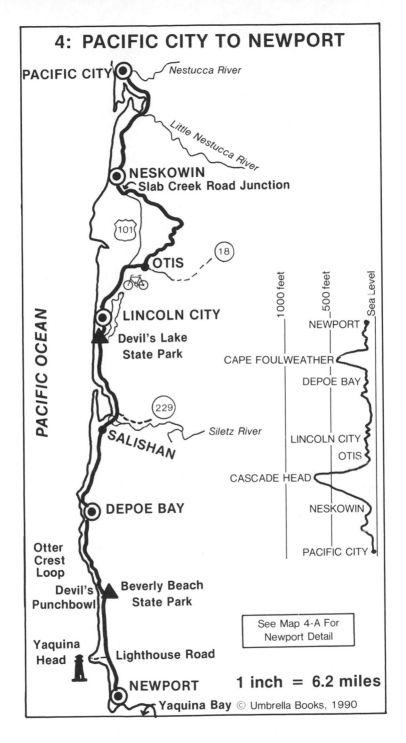

4: PACIFIC CITY TO NEWPORT

PACIFIC CITY · *Nestucca River*

Little Nestucca River

NESKOWIN
Slab Creek Road Junction

101

18

OTIS

LINCOLN CITY

Devil's Lake
State Park

229

Siletz River

SALISHAN

DEPOE BAY

Otter
Crest
Loop

Devil's
Punchbowl

Beverly Beach
State Park

Yaquina
Head

Lighthouse Road

NEWPORT

Yaquina Bay

PACIFIC OCEAN

1000 feet | 500 feet | Sea Level

NEWPORT
CAPE FOULWEATHER
DEPOE BAY

LINCOLN CITY
OTIS

CASCADE HEAD

NESKOWIN

PACIFIC CITY

See Map 4-A For
Newport Detail

1 inch = 6.2 miles

© Umbrella Books, 1990

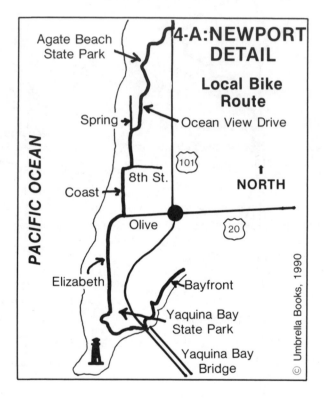

4-A: NEWPORT DETAIL

Local Bike Route

Agate Beach State Park

Spring

Ocean View Drive

PACIFIC OCEAN

101

NORTH

8th St.

Coast

Olive

20

Elizabeth

Bayfront

Yaquina Bay State Park

Yaquina Bay Bridge

© Umbrella Books, 1990

Chapter 4

PACIFIC CITY TO NEWPORT

(54 Miles)

This leg of the trip includes spectacular ocean coves, small bays, weird rocks and rugged vistas along the coast. The rewards are more than equal to the three main difficulties: Cascade Head, Lincoln City and Cape Foulweather.

The first ten miles, from Pacific City to Neskowin, offer easy biking through countryside that is more relaxing than thrilling. Cascade Head looms next as the day's most arduous climb. There's no bypassing Cascade Head, but bikers have a choice of how to mount it. We recommend the scenic route: a creek-side meander, one steep sylvan climb, and a lightly-traveled road without a shoulder. The more direct and quicker alternative route, on Highway 101, has one long climb, no scenery and heavy traffic.

The scenic route leads back to Highway 101 just north of Lincoln City, a heavily commercialized, unattractive and unavoidable seven-mile stretch. After Lincoln City, the scenery comes on. The tiny port of Depoe Bay is a beauty. After Depoe Bay, the bike route departs from Highway 101 once again to follow the breathtaking twists and turns of the Cape Foulweather-Otter Crest scenic route. From there it's easy going, often within view of the beach, to bustling Newport on Yaquina Bay.

Mile

0.0   Pacific City's stoplight. Bike south, toward Highway 101. The road picks up the Nestucca (Neh-STUCK-ah) River and curves inland along that river's estuary.

2.7   Rejoin Highway 101 South.

4.1   Cross the Little Nestucca River.

6.3   Viewpoint, mostly for Highway 101 motorists who have not seen the ocean for a while.

9.3   Neskowin (NESS-ko-win). Means "place of plenty fish."

10.4   Junction of Slab Creek Road (Scenic Route) and Highway 101. Turn left on Slab Creek Road. Follow the creek upstream. At mile 13.8, enter the Siuslaw (Sigh-OOS-law) National Forest and discover why they call this the scenic route: the course leads through cool, wind-protected, never-logged forest. At mile 15.1, cross the bridge and start the steep, 1.1-mile climb over the back shoulder of Cascade Head. At the bottom of the hill, bear left on Old Highway 101 and cross the Salmon River into Otis. Take Highway 18 West, toward the ocean and Highway 101.

Alternate Route: At the Slab Creek Road Junction (mile 10.4), it is possible to continue straight ahead on Highway 101. The climb itself is longer (2.0 miles) but more gradual than the scenic route's climb over Cascade Head. Traffic is heavy, but the shoulder is adequate. No scenery. This dull alternative cuts five miles off the trip.

22.1   Rejoin Highway 101 South.

23.4   45th Parallel: halfway between the North Pole and the Equator. Think big.

24.4   Lincoln City Visitor Information Center. McDonald's.

Lincoln City

The Visitor Center brochure says Lincoln City lies within a two-hour drive of three-fourths of Oregon's population, and a biker might be excused for thinking they all got here at once. The place is a coastal sprawl of shopping centers, restaurants, motels, stoplights, recreational vehicles and gas fumes. Seven miles of nice white beach is, for the most part, invisible from Highway 101.

Relatively recently, in 1965, the neighboring communities of Oceanlake, Delake, Nescott, Taft and Cutler City realized they had nowhere left to expand except along the coast and into each other. So they combined and chose the name Lincoln City. Civic leaders erected a statue of Abraham Lincoln (reading) on a horse (grazing) at NE 22nd and Quay Streets, one block east of Highway 101. Lincoln looks distracted, bemused, perhaps lost but unworried. The charitable inter-pretation would be that Abe is satisfied with this place and will soon dismount and go for a stroll on the beach, if he can find it.

Unlike most major Oregon coastal towns, Lincoln City is not particularly biker-friendly. For all of its commercial vigor, Lincoln City has no bike shops, and biking gets a mere one-line entry in the town brochure. Bingo, by comparison, gets a six-line entry.

Mile

26.1   Devil's Lake State Park. Just 150 yards off Highway 101, to the left, is the hiker/biker campground. Devil's Lake, which wraps around Lincoln City to the east, is a good place for freshwater fishing and swimming. The name comes from the Indians who believed that an evil spirit, or skookum, lived in the lake.

26.4   D River Wayside and ocean view. They call the D River, a 400-yard trickle from Devil's Lake to the Pacific Ocean, the world's smallest river.

30.3   Leave Lincoln City.

31.5   Kernville Junction. Highway 229 meets Highway 101.

Side Trip: Stamper House

Take Highway 229 up the tidal Siletz River just 1.4 miles. On the opposite side of the river sits the old Victorian house, now fixed up and inhabited, where they shot the movie of Ken Kesey's *Sometimes a Great Notion*. The home is not open to the public, but there's a good view of it from across the Siletz.

Another half mile upstream is Coyote Rock, a promontory into the Siletz River. According to Indian Legend, Coyote tried to push the cliff into the river here in order to dam it up and assure himself a generous supply of salmon. Coyote was only partially successful, but in fact the Chinook do hang out in deep water here before the fall rains draw them upstream to spawn. Coyote Rock is now the site of an RV campground and fishing marina.

Mile

31.7   Cross the Siletz River. Visible across the Siletz estuary, on the right, is Salishan Spit. In the early 1970s, homesites on this strip of dunes showed some of the same tendencies toward erosion as at the unlucky Bayocean Spit, near Tillamook. Now, written into the lease of each homeowner is a "rebutment requirement." At their own expense, owners must plant big boulders on their property to keep nature at bay, so to speak.

32.9   Salishan Lodge. This resort and convention center has won many architectural and landscaping awards for successfully integrating nature with man at play. Salishan, say the experts, is coastal development at its least intrusive and best.

37.6   Boiler Bay Wayside. The steam schooner *J. Marhoffer* burned, after an explosion of a gasoline torch, and drifted ashore here in 1910. The ship's boiler is still visible at low tide.

39.1   Depoe Bay Bridge.

Depoe Bay

The U.S. government, in 1894, allotted land around this tiny picture-postcard bay to William Charles DePoe, or Depoe, a Rogue River Indian. Depoe's name is said to have come from his service, as a youth, at a U.S. Army depot. The town came much later. For a long time there was no bridge. Tourists couldn't get through, and there was no overland outlet for locally-caught fish.

The Depoe Bay Bridge is one of the earliest and finest examples of the work of Conde B. McCullough, who became well-known for his ability to build bridges in harmony with marine settings. The bridge was completed in 1926 and opened to traffic in 1927. It was widened to four lanes in 1940, with an addition on the seaward side of the bridge. A stairwell on the bay side and a walkway at the north end of the bridge give access to Depoe Bay State Park.

In 1950, the U.S. Army Corps of Engineers excavated and enlarged the harbor entrance to fifty feet at its widest, five feet at its shallowest. Before the expansion, boats rode these surging waters through a mere twenty-foot opening in the bay's basalt flanks, and they could only do it at high tide. Even today, Depoe Bay is not an easy harbor to enter when seas are rough.

Atop the Made in Oregon Store, just north and west of the bridge, is a glass-enclosed viewing room. Excellent exhibits help explain the geology, hydrology and biology of the Depoe Bay area.

Mile

40.8   Whale Cove.

41.2   Turn right off Highway 101 onto Otter Crest Loop for a lower-elevation and much more scenic few miles.

CAUTION: A covering of fir or spruce needles makes the road shoulder appear firm when in fact the needles may cover bike-grabbing sand. Stay on the blacktop, or be moving slowly enough to be nearly stopped before turning off.

43.0   Cape Foulweather. Historical marker and spectacular view. On March 7, 1778, ten years before Robert Gray entered Tillamook Bay, the English Captain James Cook first sighted this promontory. He was on his way back from discovering the Sandwich (Hawaiian) Islands. The grumpy and storm-tossed Cook also gave the cape its name. Later that same day, members of his crew made landfall in smaller boats as Cook's two ships poked and parried their way south along the coast. Published accounts of Cook's sightings aroused world interest and brought Gray and others here in search of furs.

44.4   Turn right on First Street, toward Otter Rock.

44.9   Devil's Punchbowl State Park. A natural bowl at surfside was formed when the sandstone roof over two adjoining sea caves collapsed. At high tide, the surf rushes in and goes churning and foaming within the cavern walls, while tourists look down on it and take pictures. At low tide, this show is suspended, although the empty cavern is still worth a look.

       If you happen to arrive at low tide, take the trail from the north side of the park to the Marine Gardens for a good look at starfish, anemone and other colorful and temporarily exposed sea critters.

       Exit from Devil's Punchbowl State Park on First Street.

45.4   At the east end of First Street, turn right.

45.8   Rejoin Highway 101 South.

46.8   Beverly Beach State Park. Hiker/biker campground.

50.4   Lighthouse Road.

Side Trip: Yaquina Head Lighthouse

Take Lighthouse Road from Highway 101. One mile away is land's end, the tip of Yaquina (Yuh-KWIN-ah) Head.

The lighthouse was built in 1873, in the wrong place. It was meant for Cape Foulweather, three miles north. The folks who delivered the building materials around Cape Horn took one look at that godless promontory and decided that Yaquina Head would be the place to unload. The lighthouse is still operated by the U.S. Coast Guard, and it is open to the public. Since 1873 its beam has been darkened only once, after the bombing of Pearl Harbor.

Islands and rocks to the south of Yaquina Head are in Oregon Islands National Wildlife Refuge. From the observation deck, visitors watch tufted puffins, pigeon guillemots, gulls, cormorants and murres. These waters contain the whelk, a carnivrous snail that uses its sharp tongue to drill through the shell of its prey. In winter and spring, schools of gray whales can often be seen from Yaquina Head as they migrate between the Baja Peninsula and the Bering Sea.

Mile

51.1   Turn right off Highway 101 toward Agate Beach State Park.

51.5   Agate Beach State Park. The sands around Newport are well known for their agates — translucent gemstones, including jaspers. The agates wash up among the sea gravels with each fresh tide.

Follow the Oregon Coast Bike Route signs as they jog seaward and into Newport along Oceanview Drive and Spring and Coast Streets. Turn left on Olive Street to reach the commercial center.

53.7   Newport. Junction of Highways 101 and 20.

NEWPORT

We like Newport because the public library doesn't have fines. It has a Conscience Box. Put a dollar in, and the lady says, "Oh, that's too much."

Newport is a real seaport. Smell it. People make a living off the sea. Yaquina Bay hosts a fleet of big commercial trollers that are out on the Pacific for days and weeks at a time. The wharves on Bay Avenue are lined with canneries and packing houses. Here fresh fish are cleaned and crated and loaded onto refrigerator trucks for overnight delivery to inland markets. Piled on top of all this commercial activity are the tourists. Charter boats unload their customers and catch within view of slick boutiques, the fabulous Wax Museum, the unbelievable Ripley's Believe It Or Not and the amazing Undersea Gardens.

The genuine and the artificial are close allies on the Bayfront. It's fun. Night life in Newport is an odd mix of weathered sea hands and polished tourists. Everybody seems slightly out of place and off center, so bikers fit right in.

Another nice thing about Newport is the local bike route, a semi-circular cruise for two-wheelers along wide and lesser-traveled Newport streets. Pick up the route where Third Street meets Coast Street and follow the route south along the coastline toward Yaquina Bay State Park and back to the Bayfront.

The Sylvia Beach Hotel

An unusual and attractive place to stay in Newport is the Sylvia Beach Hotel, at 267 NW Cliff. This historic (1913) honeymooner haven was reopened and renamed in the 1980s as a hotel for book-lovers. Twenty guest rooms are furnished and named after individual authors—The Agatha Christie Room, The Mark Twain Room, The Colette Room ... The hotel serves hot wine at night in the library. The ocean-front restaurant here is called, "Tables of Content." Reservations are required at the restaurant, and are often necessary for a hotel room. Phone (503) 265-5428.

Sylvia Beach was a person, not a stretch of sand. In the 1920s and 1930s, she owned the Shakespeare & Co. Bookstore in Paris. She hung out with Gertrude Stein and Ernest Hemingway and other left bank expatriates.

Newport Performing Arts Center

Summer stock evening theater at the Center, 777 West Olive Street, is often preceded by a musical cabaret and light supper. Call (503) 265-ARTS to find out what's on.

Yaquina Bay State Park

The state park, just west of the north ramp to the Yaquina Bay Bridge, sits on a bluff with a commanding view of the bay and the jetties that define the mouth of the Yaquina River. Within sight of the bluff, Captain James Cook passed by on the same stormy March 7, 1778, that he had named Cape Foulweather. Although members of his crew came ashore in smaller boats, Cook was unable to find a suitable harbor for his two ships, and he continued on down the coast. News of Cook's sightings spurred Thomas Jefferson's interest and led, when Jefferson became President, to the Louisiana Purchase in 1803 and the expedition of Lewis and Clark.

Yaquina Bay bar has been the scene of many shipwrecks, the most recent of which occurred on November 19, 1983, when the storm-crippled *Blue Magpie* made a nighttime run for the safety of the bay and didn't make it. The ship—a 321-foot, Japanese-owned and Korean-operated cargo vessel—got lifted on huge swells and was deposited astraddle the tip of North Jetty, where it broke into three pieces. A Coast Guard helicopter, with the heroic cooperation of the Newport fire and police departments, rescued all nineteen crew members. In 1989, six years later, fragments of the wreck were still visible off North Jetty, but they were rapidly being claimed by the sea.

Yaquina Bay Lighthouse

The lighthouse on the grounds of Yaquina State Park is the only lighthouse on the Oregon coast with a combined keeper's dwelling and light tower. The oldest existing building in Newport, it first cast its light to guide ships into the bay in 1871. Only three years later, however, they shut it down. The light was not visible to ships approaching from the north, because of protruding headlands. A more efficient lighthouse was built at Yaquina Head.

To this day, the story persists that the lighthouse is haunted. Shortly after the light and dwelling were abandoned, a sweet-tempered young thing named Muriel Trevenard is said to have explored the empty quarters with a couple of her girlfriends. In an upper room, the girls heard a sound, panicked and fled. Muriel went back to get a handkerchief she had dropped, and her friends never saw her again. They did find the hanky, in a pool of blood on the floor. Over the next century there were several claimed sightings of Muriel Trevenard's ghost, and a current museum keeper will testify to unexplained and sudden temperature changes within the building.

Don't miss the twenty-minute video they show at the lighthouse museum. It not only recreates the ghost story but also has footage of the wreck of the *Blue Magpie*, including taped radio transmissions between the Coast Guard and the stricken ship.

Yaquina Bay Bridge and C.B. McCullough

The graceful, high-arching bridge over Newport's bay is one of five major spans completed in 1936 during the federally-assisted Works Progress Administration Oregon Coast Bridges project. All five were designed by Conde Balcom McCullough, and the bike route will cross all five of them in the next two days. The other bridges cross Alsea Bay at Waldport, the Siuslaw River at Florence, the Umpqua River at Reedsport, and Coos Bay at North Bend. McCullough (1887-1946) headed the civil engineering department at Oregon State University before he joined the state highway department in 1919. By the time of the Coastal Bridges project, McCullough—whose engineering skill was matched by his artistry—had already designed the celebrated bridges at Depoe Bay (1927), Cape Creek (1931) and Rogue River (1931). His big series of bridges in 1936 essentially completed U.S. Highway 101 by eliminating the need for ferry crossings at major river mouths and bays.

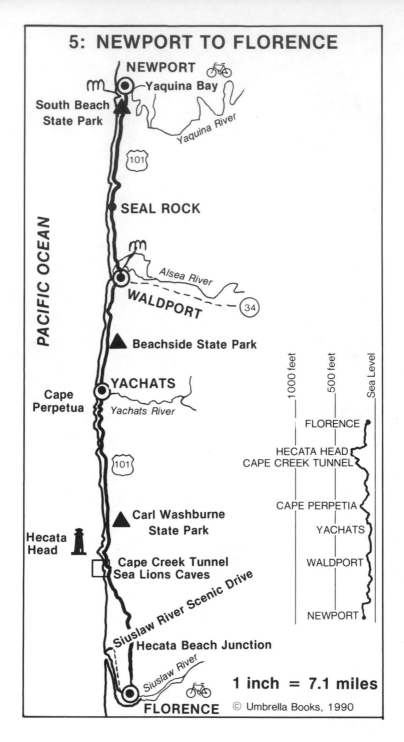

5: NEWPORT TO FLORENCE

NEWPORT

Yaquina Bay

South Beach
State Park

Yaquina River

{101}

PACIFIC OCEAN

SEAL ROCK

Alsea River

WALDPORT

(34)

▲ **Beachside State Park**

YACHATS

Cape
Perpetua

Yachats River

{101}

▲ **Carl Washburne
State Park**

Hecata
Head

**Cape Creek Tunnel
Sea Lions Caves**

Siuslaw River Scenic Drive

Hecata Beach Junction

Siuslaw River

1 inch = 7.1 miles

FLORENCE   © Umbrella Books, 1990

1000 feet | 500 feet | Sea Level

FLORENCE

HECATA HEAD
CAPE CREEK TUNNEL

CAPE PERPETIA

YACHATS

WALDPORT

NEWPORT

44

Chapter 5

NEWPORT TO FLORENCE

(50 Miles)

This demanding and rewarding leg of the trip begins deceptively with a series of low undulations on Highway 101 out of Newport. The ocean is close but mostly out of sight. Salal, thimbleberry and wind-sculpted sea pines top the road cuts, which reveal sandstone in the making. At Seal Rock the highway opens to ocean views and asks little biking effort in return. Waldport to Yachats is a piece of cake. Then the fun begins. Not with a bang but with a slow crescendo.

The course rises gradually out of Yachats to skirt Cape Perpetua on the ocean side. The road doesn't climb very high, but its shoulder narrows on tight curves. This section is what recalls the earlier warning that the coastal route is not for kids, not for novice bikers, not for anyone with a short attention span.

After beautiful Cape Perpetua comes a ten-mile breather with wide shoulders and continuing excellent views. Next comes the two-headed Heceta Head. The double climb includes a tunnel, Sea Lion caves and wonderful ocean vistas. Never, on this leg, does the road rise above 400 feet elevation. But there's a fine feeling of accomplishment that comes with the ride. Blitzing down off Heceta Head toward Florence, a biker has *earned* this piece of coast.

Mile

0.0   Newport. Junction of Highways 101 and 20.

1.0   Yaquina Bay Bridge. Walk the bike on pedestrian sidewalk.

1.7   Turnoff to the Mark O. Hatfield Marine Science Center, less than a mile from Highway 101, on Yaquina Bay. The Center is home to Oregon State University's coastal research, teaching and extension work. The chief attraction for visitors is the aquarium. On the periphery of clean and modern aquarial tanks are exhibits on marine archeology and geology, estuaries, tides and the circulation of ocean currents. It's a wonderfully compact and educational display of how the ocean works. Docked nearby, if it's in port, is the National Science Foundation's 177-foot research vessel, *The Wecoma*. The Center is open every day of the week, but not until 9:30 A.M.

3.0   South Beach State Park. The hiker/biker campground is half a mile seaward from Highway 101.

10.1 Seal Rock. This one-street, no-stoplight town has groceries, cafes and wood carvers. On most summer mornings there are live performances of chainsaw art right next to the highway.

14.9 Alsea Bay Bridge. Walk the bike on pedestrian sidewalk.

15.6 Waldport. Junction of Highways 101 and 34.

Waldport

Alsea (AL-see) Bay takes its name from the Indian word *Alsi,* meaning peace. The Germans came in and called the place Waldport, meaning woods-port. Waldport was once a lumber exporting center, but today it is chiefly a fishing port. Waldport isn't the only town that dubs itself the Salmon Fishing Capital of the World, but that tag has some merit. Annual runs of salmon, steelhead and sea-run cutthroat trout keep the docks crawling with sport fishermen. Alsea Bay is also a good place to gather Dungeness crab, razor clams, mud clams, horsenecks and cockles.

Waldport's most striking man-made visual feature is the Alsea Bay Bridge, one of the famous spans designed by C.B. McCullough along the Oregon Coast. Long (over half a mile) and graceful, the bridge cost less than a million dollars in 1936. Although its design was inspired, its construction was flawed. There was too much saltwater in the concrete mix, they say, and the bridge is crumbling. A three-year project to build a new Alsea Bay Bridge, at a cost of $35 million, began in 1989. The new bridge will be lower, with four traffic lanes and wide sidewalks. It will be safer for bikers, but not nearly so beautiful. The old bridge, sadly, will be torn down when the new bridge is finished, in the summer of 1991.

Mile

19.0   Beachside State Park. Hiker/biker campground.

23.2   Entering Yachats (YAH-hots).

23.3   Turnoff to Smelt Sands State Park. Unpaved Lemwick Lane dead-ends one fifth of a mile off Highway 101 at a beach of fine gravel, not exactly "sands," where silver smelt spawn. In 1948, aroused citizens of Yachats protested the removal of this scarce and unusual beach gravel for commercial use in building roads and mixing concrete.

The State Highway Commission had given a private company a permit to scrape gravel off the beach. Echoing the words of ex-governor Oswald West — "The beaches belong to the people" — the angry locals enlisted the support of newspaper editorial writers all over the state. The resulting uproar led to preservation of this area for public use and for the propagation of the rare silver smelt.

23.4   Turn right off Highway 101 onto Marine Drive for the scenic route through the small town of Yachats. Take a left on Oceanview and curve with the shoreline back to Highway 101.

YACHATS

The Chamber of Commerce translates the Indian word Yachats as "Dark waters at the foot of the mountains," which is a big load for so few phonemes. But it certainly is a lovely spot. Surf comes muffled into the sleepy green waters of the Yachats River. Nearby homes and summer cottages feel rich and settled, quietly confident.

Little Log Church by the Sea

At Third and Pontiac Streets sits a gem of a log church that was built in 1927 when Yachats citizens of all denominations donated time and material for a community place of worship. The building was donated in 1968 to the Lincoln County Historical Society for use as a museum. Photos along one wall document the construction of the first road around Cape Perpetua, a narrow scar that the U.S. Forest Service blasted into the rock in 1914. The museum has a picture of Cy Cooper and his 1918 Model T Ford, in which Cooper delivered mail along the coast south of Yachats. The Ford's specially-adapted transmission and rear axle gave Cooper thirteen forward and eight reverse gears. He is said to have started shifting gears at Yachats and didn't finish shifting until he neared Florence.

Museum scrapbooks include a story written by Ann Lossner in the *Keizer Times* about Delbert Blair, who was five years old in 1926 when his family came to the coast in a Mercer touring car. The family "had to drive around Cape Perpetua on a one-lane, winding, scary road built into the side of the cliff. Frightened, Delbert's mother and aunt took their children out of the car and let Delbert's father drive the loaded car over the perilous road by himself, while they walked."

A widened Highway 101 was completed around Cape Perpetua in 1935. It has been improved since then, but the route still calls for caution.

Mile

24.9   Cross the Yachats River.

26.1   CAUTION: From here to the road summit on Cape Perpetua, the grade steepens and the shoulder slims. The big recreational vehicles can't give bikers as much room as everybody would like. Be alert.

26.7   Road summit (western-most bend) on Cape Perpetua. The British explorer James Cook, on his return from Hawaii and just after naming Cape Foulweather, is the first to have recorded sighting this rocky headland, in March of 1778. After five days trying to sail past the cape on a storm-tossed sea, the intrepid but increasingly gloomy Cook made this entry in his journal on March 11: "The Northern [point] was the same which we had first seen on the seventh; and on that account I called it 'Cape Perpetua.'"

27.1   Devil's Churn Viewpoint. In the battle between ocean and land, Devil's Churn is the opposite of a headland. The sea has attacked a narrow soft spot in the basalt to drive a liquid slit into the oceanside cliffs. Here the continent is holding its own, but the surf's powerful cutting action is dramatically on display.

27.5   Cape Perpetua Visitors Center. The U.S. Forest Service screens an excellent fifteen-minute film, *Discovery at the Edge*, about the geology and hydrology of headland capes. The film explains the massive basalt uprising that is Cape Perpetua, and how the sea eats away softer rock first to leave sea stacks, caves and spouting horns.

Across Highway 101 from the Visitor Center, a footpath leads two hundred yards to Indian middens. Middens are huge piles of seashells. Middens are ancient garbage dumps, to be blunt about it. Archeologists learn a lot from middens. Even a non-professional can find it intriguing to stand facing the sea on one of these huge mounds, now grass-covered, and think about the appetite of those native Americans who camped and fished and gathered shellfish here over a thousand years ago.

29.5   Strawberry Hill Wayside. Watch harbor seals on rocks.

31.2   Sea Perch Grocery.

35.6   Muriel O. Ponsler Memorial Wayside, with beach access and a
        view south to Heceta Head. Jack C. Ponsler donated this
        property in his wife's memory in 1939 for public use and
        enjoyment.

36.2   Carl G. Washburne State Park. Hiker/biker campground.

38.3   Devil's Elbow State Park. The best reason to pull off Highway
        101 here is to see the Cape Creek Bridge from below. Opened
        to traffic in 1932, this beauty is another of those bridges designed
        by C.B. McCullough, the famous Oregon state highway en-
        gineer. The bridge's two-tiered arches and columns look like a
        Roman aqueduct over the rugged Cape Creek canyon.

        From the park, a footpath leads to Heceta Light and Heceta
        House, which are described below. Both are open to the public.

38.4   Cross the Cape Creek Bridge.

38.6   Cape Creek Tunnel.

        CAUTION: Pull off before the tunnel entrance, and rest for a
        moment. When you're ready, push the button to activate the
        yellow flashing lights. Then pedal like mad. The tunnel is less
        than a quarter mile long, and its end is visible from the start.

39.1   The third viewpoint after the tunnel is the best place to stop and
        look back on picturesque Heceta Head. The name comes from
        the Spanish navigator Bruno de Hezeta (ay-THAY-tah). In
        1775 he sailed up the coast from Mexico and noted the features
        of this promontory. Now his name is spelled Heceta, and most
        coastal residents pronounce it Ha-SEE-tah.

        Heceta Light first cast its beam over the ocean in 1894. The light
        was automated in 1963, but it still operates with the original
        rotating Fresnel lens. The lighthouse, bright white against the

dark green of the cape, not only makes a pretty picture but also shows up from sea as a daytime landmark. The stately Queen Anne duplex near the light is Heceta House, the former home of the lightkeepers' families. In 1893 the lumber for Heceta House was delivered offshore, thrown overboard, and snatched from the surf by the builders.

39.4   Sea Lion Caves. America's largest sea cave is home to the Stellar sea lion, an enormous eared seal. Bulls run 1,200 to 1,500 pounds. This is the breed's only mainland rookery from California to the Bering Sea. Elsewhere, they live on offshore rocks. The sea lions that occupy this cave will stay here all year long — in the cave during winter and storms, and outside in spring and summer. Sea Lion Caves has been private property since Captain William Cox discovered the site and bought it from the state in 1887. Today Sea Lion Caves is a business. It costs more than lunch to take the elevator down to the cave to view sea lions, but do it. The cave is unique, and the smell is unforgettable. After visiting the cave, you might not *need* lunch.

40.1   Road summit. Accept a biker's reward: the thrilling descent off Heceta Head. Ahead lie wide-open views of sweeping white sands. The jetty in the south distance guards the Siuslaw (Sigh-OOS-law) River, near Florence.

45.3   Darlingtonia Botanical Gardens. Just a hundred yards to the left of Highway 101 is a spooky bog full of *Darlingtonia californica*, commonly known as pitcher plants or cobra lilies. These carnivorous plants lure and trap insects, and digest them as food. A short footpath into the woods leads to a viewing platform, which is always open.

47.4   Heceta Beach Junction.

50.4   Florence. Junction of Highways 101 and 126.

FLORENCE

Some of the best legends are hard to believe. This one has to do with two beachcombing Siuslaw Indians who came across a slab of flotsam with writing on it. They took it to the town's first hotel owner for a translation. The wood was the nameplate of a French sailing vessel, the *Florence*, which wrecked near the mouth of the Siuslaw River in 1873. The hotel owner, intrigued, hung the slab over the door to his hotel, and the town was thereafter called Florence.

Historians—those sticks in the mud—point out that the town was probably named for H.B. Florence, who was Lane County's representative to the Oregon State Senate from 1858 to 1860.

The Siuslaw Indians fished and hunted this area in relatively uncomplicated and undisturbed ways until the arrival in 1824 of A.R. McCleod, a Hudson's Bay Co. trapper. Soon the word about furs was out. In 1852 the Indians signed a treaty that reserved for the tribe 2.5 million acres of heavily timbered land. But the tribe of some three thousand was nearly eliminated by the smallpox epidemic of 1870. When less than four hundred tribal members remained, the U.S. drastically reduced the size of the reservation and opened the area to white settlers in 1876.

A rough corduroy log road to Eugene was finished in 1883, but Florence's highway of commerce was primarily the Siuslaw River and the Pacific Ocean. At the turn of the century, Florence was the hub of central coast fishing and lumber industries. Chinese cannery workers cleaned and sliced the fish, cut the metal to form cans, filled them with steaming salmon and soldered the lids shut. Most of the lumber went to San Francisco by sea.

Today Florence has a year-around population of 19,000, about half of whom are retired. The area features good fishing, not only in the ocean and river, but also in many nearby freshwater lakes. Highway 101 leading into town could be Anywhere, U.S.A., but Florence's Old Town is a cozy and scaled-down version of Newport's, a nice riverside spot to end a day's bike ride.

Old Town

Three blocks of Bay Street, near the north ramp of the Siuslaw River Bridge, include shops and restaurants and access to the piers and marinas used by the Florence fishing fleet. At Bay and Laurel Streets is the miniature Old Town Park, with a gazebo at the head of a walkway down to a platform-like dock. The dock is a popular place for fishing or crabbing, or just to eat a snack and take in the view and swirling tides. The Siuslaw River Bridge (1936) is another example of C.B. McCullough's genius. Stark white sand dunes on the opposite shore fall steeply and abruptly to river's edge.

Kyle Building

In 1901 William Kyle built the first general store in Florence, on Bay Street. This white plank, false-fronted, Italianate structure is still standing and now houses the Bridgewater Restaurant and Oyster Bar. On weekend evenings a local three-piece jazz group performs in the Patio Room.

Siuslaw Scenic Drive

With time and energy to spare in Florence, a biker does well to take a side trip along the Siuslaw River to its mouth, 5.2 miles away. The trip to the north jetty is flat and easy, unless the winds are up. From under the bridge at Bay Street, zig and zag westward as close to the Siuslaw River as possible to reach a T and a stop sign at Rhododendron Street. Rhododendron bends north with the river and goes past the Coast Guard station to Harbor Vista Park. Take North Jetty Road to its end. The U.S. Army Corps of Engineers extended both jetties of the Siuslaw River in the 1980s. Trucks carrying the boulders logged over two million miles to finish the project.

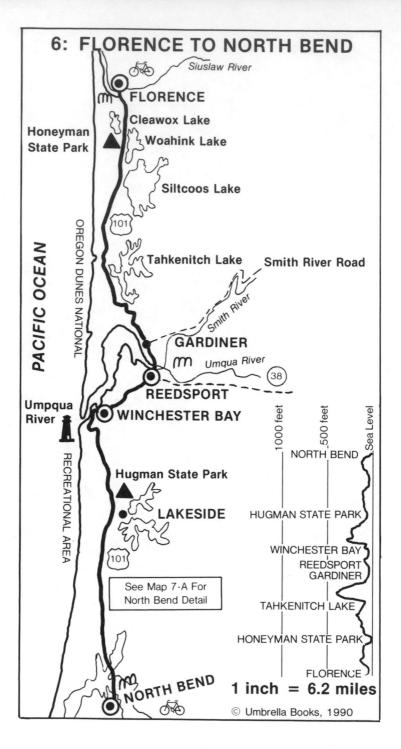

6: FLORENCE TO NORTH BEND

Siuslaw River

FLORENCE

Cleawox Lake

Honeyman
State Park

Woahink Lake

Siltcoos Lake

US 101

PACIFIC OCEAN

OREGON DUNES NATIONAL

Tahkenitch Lake

Smith River Road

Smith River

GARDINER

Umqua River

38

REEDSPORT

Umpqua
River

WINCHESTER BAY

RECREATIONAL AREA

Hugman State Park

1000 feet

500 feet

Sea Level

NORTH BEND

LAKESIDE

HUGMAN STATE PARK

WINCHESTER BAY

REEDSPORT
GARDINER

US 101

TAHKENITCH LAKE

See Map 7-A For
North Bend Detail

HONEYMAN STATE PARK

FLORENCE

NORTH BEND

1 inch = 6.2 miles

© Umbrella Books, 1990

Chapter 6

FLORENCE TO COOS BAY

(47 Miles)

Huge sand dunes dominate the coastline between Florence and Coos Bay. In 1972, Congress created the Oregon Dunes National Recreation Area to preserve a stretch of sand forty miles long and up to three miles wide. The area was turned over to black-tailed deer, coyotes, sand beetles, bobcats and—in designated sections—horseback riders and dune-buggy drivers.

In theory, dunes are really interesting. Glacial grinding and river runoff, over the millennia, washed particles of continental rock out to sea, where they got swirled around and ground even finer into sand. The wind and marine currents sweep the sand southward in summer and northward in winter. Outward sand-flow has slowed to a trickle, but tide and wind still move the sand around. The current brings it to the beach. The wind piles the sand into dunes sometimes five hundred feet high.

In practice, sand dunes are among the least compelling things a biker can encounter. Can't bike 'em. Can't even see 'em, much, from Highway 101. Writ large, as they are here, the dunes hide the ocean from view. A recent informal poll of bikers elicited the widely shared sentiment that dunes are a darn nuisance. "If you've seen one sand dune," says one biker, "you've seen them all."

Highlights of this leg of the coastal route are bunched at the middle, from historic Gardiner to the lighthouse and museum at the mouth of the Umpqua River. Sandwiched around those highlights are the day's two major climbs, the first one from Tahkenitch Lake and the second one from Umpqua Lighthouse State Park. At the end comes a bike-walk across the tall and scary Coos Bay Bridge.

Mile

0.0   Florence. Junction of Highways 101 and 126.

0.6   Cross the Siuslaw River Bridge.

1.7   Siuslaw Pioneer Museum. This barn-shaped structure, originally a Lutheran Church and later a pizza parlor, became a museum in 1974. Stained-glass windows filter colored light onto pioneer furnishings and Indian artifacts that include a fine old dugout canoe, and stone and bone tools.

2.2   Morgan's Country Kitchen is a solid breakfast place, frequented by locals as well as by the touring crowd.

3.2   Honeyman State Park. Hiker/biker campground. For those who don't believe everything they read and simply must climb a sand dune, this is a handy access point. The park's Cleawox (KLEE-ah-wox) Lake is a good swimming hole.

4.4   Sand Dunes Frontier, Inc. offers dune buggy rides.

10.6   Oregon Dunes Overlook, a quarter of a mile off Highway 101.

12.5   Tahkenitch (TAW-keh-nitch) Lake. The Indian word Tahkenitch is said to mean "many arms." The lake's irregular shape gives it 113 miles of shoreline.

14.1   Begin a 1.4-mile gradual climb.

15.5   Road summit.

18.9 Gardiner. Big mills of the International Paper Co. and Bohemia Inc. continue the wood-products tradition of Gardiner. The town was named for a Boston merchant whose schooner, *Bostonian,* wrecked on the Umpqua River bar in 1850. Salvaged cargo was brought ashore here, and soon a logging camp and sawmills fed the brisk coastal sailing trade. Wilson Jewett, owner of the Gardiner Mill Co., gave Gardiner the nickname "White City" by donating lumber and white paint to rebuild the town after fires in 1880, 1911 and 1915.

Wilson Jewett's home (built in 1908) is opposite the historical marker on Highway 101. Jewett built its gingerbread neighbor for his son. Loop back on Front Street for a sampling of Gardiner's many historical structures. Above the town, on the hill, sits the tiny, white, wood-frame Episcopal Church of St. Mary the Virgin.

20.1 Cross the Smith River.

20.6 Historical Marker. Jedediah Smith was a mountain man, a God-serving American trapper, whose place in frontier history was assured by his ability to walk. Smith had walked from Missouri to the Rockies any number of times before his curiosity led him to walk to the missions in southern California. From there he explored thickly overgrown and nearly impenetrable western coasts and rivers on foot. Smith and a party of seventeen trappers camped near this spot on July 13, 1828. The next morning, Smith and two others set forth to find a crossing over the river that now bears his name. While he was gone, Indians massacred all but one man in camp. Smith and the survivors then walked to Fort Vancouver (near present-day Portland). The generous John McLoughlin, administrator of the Hudson's Bay Co. in Vancouver, resupplied Smith with the men and means to walk back to the Umpqua and recover some of his furs.

20.7 Umpqua River Bridge. Another in the series of 1936 bridges designed by C.B. McCullough, this is the biggest swing-span structure in Oregon. Walk the bike on the pedestrian sidewalk.

21.3 Reedsport. Junction of Highways 101 and 38.

REEDSPORT

The railroad from Eugene and the Willamette Valley estabished its Umpqua River-mouth terminal here in 1916, thereby allowing Reedsport to leapfrog the neighboring towns of Winchester Bay and Gardiner as the area's commercial hub. Sailing schooners and paddle-wheel river steamers were the chief mode of commerce and passenger service before the railroad. Today Reedsport arranges itself linearly along Highway 101 to feed and lodge fishermen, dune-players and sightseers on their way up and down the coast. Lumber is still the principal industry.

Oregon Dunes National Recreation Area Headquarters

The Siuslaw National Forest has its dunes information center at the junction of Highways 101 and 38. These U.S. Forest Service people really get into it. They have their foredunes, their hummocks, their traverse dunes, their oblique dunes, their parabola dunes. They show a video. They know far more about sand than a biker, or a golfer, would ever want to know.

Dean Creek Elk Viewing Station

Three miles east of Highway 101 on Highway 38 (good shoulder, one mild hump and pleasant river views) is a wide meadow where Roosevelt elk emerge from the woods to feed. These elk are wild, but they are protected from hunting. Elk stay here all year long. Can the elk be relied upon to make themselves visible, if you bike out there? "Usually," says one local resident who regularly travels Highway 38. "More often than not," says another. "I'd say three-quarters of the time. If you get there in late September, October, you might even hear them bugling. Before they rut." To help decide whether or not to bike out there, check at the Forest Service headquarters or ask motorists arriving at the Highway 38 stop light if the elk are in sight today.

> **Alternate Route:** At mile 25.6, it is safe to stay on Highway 101 South to begin a long climb. This is the official Oregon Coast Bike Route, which cuts a mile and a half off the route we recommend. Highway 101 has a long (1.5-mile) gradual climb instead of a shorter and steeper one, but it misses Salmon Harbor and some fine river and ocean views. It also misses a lighthouse and a neat little museum.

Mile

25.6   Winchester Bay. Turn right on Beach Boulevard toward Windy Cove Parks.

25.8   Salmon Harbor, on the right. This is the largest recreational salmon port on the Oregon coast.

25.9   Bear left at the Y. The road borders the Umpqua River and Half Moon Bay.

26.8   Turn left and climb a short hill toward the lighthouse.

27.2   Coastal Visitor Center. Museum. This three-story building built in (1939) once served as bachelor quarters for the Coast Guardsmen who manned the lighthouse and the local lifesaving station. The Coast Guard still has an active lifesaving station here, with headquarters near the lighthouse, but they employ fewer people these days because the jetties and modern navigation techniques have made the Umpqua River bar a safer place for boats.

Douglas County has restored the old building for use as a museum. It has pictures of sailing schooners lined up at the Gardiner Mill Co. wharves. The era of stern-wheel river steamers is well-documented. The museum shows the history of the local lifesaving station, and the evolution of rescue craft. It also documents the construction of Fort Umpqua in 1856 to protect settlers and lighthouse builders from unfriendly Indians.

27.4   Umpqua River Lighthouse and Viewpoint. The view is of
        the entrance to the Umpqua River, with its jetties extending
        seaward. Before these jetties stabilized the river mouth, many
        ships were lost crossing the bar.

        The first lighthouse in the Oregon Territory was begun in 1855,
        downhill from the current lighthouse and viewpoint, near the
        river mouth. Lower Umpqua Indians harassed the builders of
        that original lighthouse by stealing materials and supplies.
        Under armed guard, the lighthouse was finally finished in 1857.
        Only five years later, high water undermined the light's sandy
        base and toppled it. So they put up another lighthouse, here on
        the bluff. The "new" lighthouse was finished in 1892. Barbier &
        Cie., in Paris, hand-cut the one thousand prisms in the light's
        huge Fresnel lens. Technical and financial hang-ups delayed the
        first lighting until 1894. The lighthouse interior is closed, except
        to groups and by appointment.

27.6   Umpqua Lighthouse State Park. Start the steep climb back to
        Highway 101.

28.0   Stop sign. Turn right toward North Bend.

28.5   Rejoin Highway 101 South.

28.7   Road summit. Viewpoint.

32.8   Tugman State Park. Hiker/biker campground.

33.5   Turnoff to Lakeside. One mile off Highway 101, to the left, is a
        small town with groceries and cafes at the shore of Tenmile
        Lake.

38.6   Wagon Wheel Grocery.

45.0   Start McCullough Bridge, over the bay called Coos. The bridge was completed in 1936 and dedicated posthumously in 1947 to honor its designer, C.B. McCullough.

CAUTION: The height and length of the bridge make it a nasty place for wind gusts. Also, the log truck drivers are apt to be impatient as they near the mills. Stay out of their way. Walk the bike on the pedestrian sidewalk.

46.0   End of bridge.

46.3   North Bend Visitor Information Center. Coos County Historical Museum.

46.6   North Bend. Junction of Highway 101 and Florida Avenue.

NORTH BEND/COOS BAY

The place names are a little confusing. Coos Bay is a bay. Coos Bay is also a town, contiguous with the town of North Bend. Coos Bay—the town—used to be known as Marshfield. Marshfield was neither a very flattering nor a very accurate description of the townsite, so the citizenry voted in 1944 to change its name to Coos Bay. Today Coos Bay—the bay with its two big towns—is the world's largest lumber shipping port.

The Bay Area Chamber of Commerce calls the area the "Lumber Supplier to the Nation." Many of the huge ships lined up at Coos Bay docks, however, are loading logs destined for Japan. It's a sore point here. Timber supply is dwindling, and many of the best logs go directly overseas, bypassing Northwest mills.

The Coos and Coquille Indians pretty much had the run of the place until well into the nineteenth century. Hudson's Bay Co. trappers took a look in 1824 and decided there were too few beaver to exploit. Jedediah Smith walked through in 1828 and didn't come back. The friendly Indians continued to live well off salmon, elk, crabs, berries and roots until Captain Asa Simpson led a white settlement to North Bend in 1853. The Simpson family started a hugely successful lumbering and shipbuilding dynasty that shaped twentieth century development of the bay area.

Less famous than the Simpsons but every bit as interesting is Verne Gorst, who introduced taxi service in 1912 by charging a quarter for a ride in his automobile from North Bend over the hill to Marshfield. Gorst and a friend, in 1914, put an auto chassis on pontoons and went skimming about the bay with a propeller aft. By 1926 the inventive and resourceful Gorst was running a coastal air mail service out of Seattle. Bay area captains of industry backed Gorst's fledgling commercial airway ventures up and down the coast that later became part of United Airlines.

Maybe there is something Gorst-like in the bay area gene pool that gives rise to exceptional individuals. Mel Counts, one of the first seven-footers who could really play basketball, graduated from Marshfield High School in 1960. Counts starred fnr the Oregon State Beavers, and later played for the Boston Celtics. Then there was Coos Bay's Steve Prefontaine. At the time of his death in a car wreck in 1975, Prefontaine held American running records in the 2,000 meters, 3,000 meters, 5,000 meters, 10,000 meters, 2 miles, 3 miles and 6 miles.

Coos County Historical Museum

A 1922 steam locomotive marks the entrance to the museum on North Bend's Sherman Street (Highway 101) at Simpson Park. Native American basketry and beadwork are on display here, as is gear from the era of steam-donkey logging and shipbuilding. The museum has a few choice relics of the *Roosevelt Ferry*, which carried trucks, cars and pedestrians across the bay until the McCullough Bridge opened in 1936. One of the museum's best exhibits features scale models of all eight lighthouses on the Oregon coast, including some that are unapproachable by bicycle, with special attention to the construction of Cape Arago Light Station on an offshore rock.

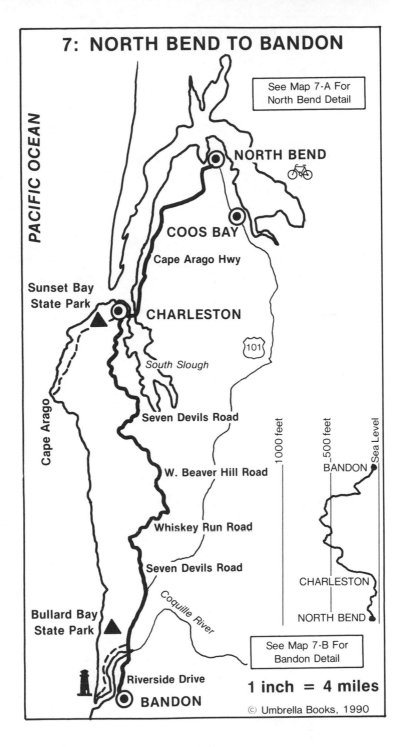

7: NORTH BEND TO BANDON

See Map 7-A For
North Bend Detail

PACIFIC OCEAN

NORTH BEND

COOS BAY

Cape Arago Hwy

Sunset Bay
State Park

CHARLESTON

101

South Slough

Cape Arago

Seven Devils Road

W. Beaver Hill Road

1000 feet

500 feet

Sea Level

BANDON

Whiskey Run Road

Seven Devils Road

Coquille River

CHARLESTON

NORTH BEND

Bullard Bay
State Park

See Map 7-B For
Bandon Detail

Riverside Drive

1 inch = 4 miles

BANDON

© Umbrella Books, 1990

65

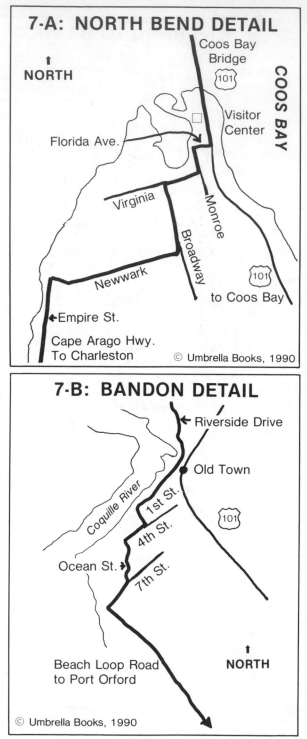

7-A: NORTH BEND DETAIL

Coos Bay Bridge

101

↑ NORTH

COOS BAY

Visitor Center

Florida Ave.

Virginia

Monroe

Broadway

Newmark

101

to Coos Bay

←Empire St.

Cape Arago Hwy.
To Charleston

© Umbrella Books, 1990

7-B: BANDON DETAIL

←Riverside Drive

Coquille River

● Old Town

1st St.

4th St.

101

Ocean St. →

7th St.

Beach Loop Road
to Port Orford

↑ NORTH

© Umbrella Books, 1990

Chapter 7

COOS BAY TO BANDON

(31 Miles)

This leg leaves the bustle of Highway 101 for a quieter trek over the old coast road between Coos Bay and Bandon. The ride to the old seaport town of Charleston jogs west and south through North Bend and picks up the Cape Arago Highway, a flat and good-shouldered course with views of the bay on the right.

Immediately after Charleston begins a tough climb up Seven Devils Road. Aside from some scattered houses, this section of the trip has few signs of civilization. No stores. No mills. Few big trucks or recreational vehicles, for a change. It's not exactly a mesa over the back shoulder of Cape Arago, but there are no long climbs after the steep grade out of Charleston.

Whiskey Run Road is a curving downhill sprint back toward the ocean. Then ride a flat but a bit rough surface back out to rejoin Highway 101 and glide into Bandon.

This chapter covers a shorter leg than some of the others. The route can easily and rewardingly be extended with a side trip to Cape Arago and three magnificent state parks, or to the Coquille River Lighthouse near Bandon.

Mile

0.0   North Bend. Junction of Highway 101 and Florida Avenue. Head west on Florida and follow Oregon Coast Bike Route signs through town:

0.2   Turn left on Monroe.

0.6   Turn right on Virginia.

1.1   Turn left on Broadway.

2.1   Turn right on Newmark.

4.1   Turn left on Empire, which becomes Cape Arago (AIR-ago) Highway. After a sorry stretch of trailer courts and second-hand stores, the road opens to nice views of the back bay.

8.6   Cross the South Slough Bridge on xylophone-like wooden sidewalk. Take in the rich seaport smells of Charleston Harbor.

8.9   Charleston Visitor Center. Groceries, cafes and old general store. Take Boat Basin Drive for a loop of Charleston Harbor.

CHARLESTON HARBOR

Follow Boat Basin Drive for 0.4 mile and turn right on Guano Rock Boulevard for another half mile to reach the center of Charleston's fishing activity. Charleston is a tradition-rich salmon-fishing port nestled into a protected nook of Coos Bay. Commercial and sport fishing boats are readily visible from raised roadways near the docks, where they unload their catch. The Sea Basket Restaurant, within view of the docks, serves fresh-caught salmon steaks and other seafood delicacies that come straight off the boats. The Sea Basket also serves up a hearty fisherman's breakfast.

At low tide, clammers dig for littlenecks, butter clams and cockles in the mudflats near the docks. The local clam specialty at Charleston is the Gaper, or Empire Clam. For those who have the time and inclination but not the gear, clamming shovels can be rented at most of the bait and tackle shops. No license is required. Ask at one of the dockside restaurants if they'll cook for you what you catch. Usually this can be negotiated for a small fee and a big tip.

Charleston Fishwives Library

At the corner of Guano Rock Boulevard and Kingfisher Drive, a small blue wooden building houses the Charleston Fishwives Library. This reading room, with easy chairs and two walls lined with well-used paperbacks, was dedicated in 1973 to the memory of Margaret E. Wick, founder and first president of Charleston Commercial Fishwives, Inc. Doña Ash, current president of the Fishwives, explains that the group was founded in 1972 to give financial and emotional support to the families of commercial fishermen lost at sea. Proceeds from cookbook sales go into the emergency fund. "Fortunately we haven't had a real disaster for the last couple of years," says Ash, "but at one time we had seven different families we were helping." Can a biker take a book from the library? "Oh goodness, yes," says Ash. "Take what you want. Read it. If you don't have a book to trade or leave, somebody else will. People are always bringing in books."

After looping the harbor area, return to the Cape Arago Highway via Boat Basin Road.

Mile

10.3   Cape Arago Highway (Charleston Visitor Center).

WARNING: This is the last chance for food and drink until Bandon. Don't leave Charleston hungry or thirsty.

10.6   Seven Devils Road junction. Turn left. The next mile has two short but very steep climbs. Once you achieve altitude (about 400 feet), there are more troughs and hills but no sustained climbs as the route crosses the back side of Cape Arago. The road flattens out as it continues south.

Side Trip: Scenic Spur—Three Parks

For a scenic five-mile visit to a terrific trio of state parks, continue on the Cape Arago Highway at mile 10.6 instead of turning off on Seven Devils Road.

Mile (from Seven Devils Road junction)

2.7   Sunset Bay. Steep sandstone bluffs protect a gentle, sandy-beach cove where the surf is mild enough, and the water sometimes warm enough, for swimming. Jedediah Smith, when he walked through in 1828, found an encampment of more than a hundred Coos Indians here. It's easy to see why; the cove's shelter and Hawaii-like beauty are just right for a clambake, if not a luau.

2.9   Sunset Bay State Park. Hiker/biker campground.

3.9   Shore Acres State Park. The botanical gardens are left over from the magnificent estate of lumberman Louis Simpson, son of North Bend-founder Asa Simpson. The sumptuous and fragrant formal gardens include a Japanese garden and a softball field-sized lily pond. A glass-enclosed observation shelter displays old photos of the place, which once had a three-story mansion complete with indoor swimming pool. Hard financial times led the Simpson family to sell the property to the state in 1942 for public use. The mansion had deteriorated too far to be saved, so it was destroyed.

4.9   Viewpoint. An island on nearby Simpson Reef hosts a village of sea lions that are clearly visible – and audible – from here.

5.4   Cape Arago State Park. From the turnaround viewpoint on this rugged headland opens a splendid panoramic view southward toward Bandon and day's end.

The only exit from this scenic spur is to retrace bike tracks back to Seven Devils Road junction.

Mile

14.8   South Slough Interpretive Center. A quarter of a mile off the
        road is an overlook toward the South Slough (of Coos Bay)
        National Estuarine Sanctuary. The Center has exhibits and films
        about the slough, which has escaped commercial development
        and is now a research center. Trailheads (not for bikes) lead
        down to the slough.

16.8   The main road bends left and changes its name from Seven
        Devils Road to West Beaver Hill Road. Continue south on West
        Beaver Hill Road.

21.4   Turn right on Whiskey Run Road toward Whiskey Run Beach
        and Seven Devils Wayside. Payoff time. Here's where bikers
        collect on their earlier investment in altitude. The curving ride
        down the hill toward sea level is a zinger, a free-wheeler, but
        watch out for potholes. The road surface is not as uniform and
        smooth as Highway 101.

23.8   Stop sign. Four corners. Turn left (south) on Seven Devils Road.

NOTE TO NORTHBOUND TRAVELERS: Do not continue
north on Seven Devils Road. The track looks good from here,
but it soon disintegrates into gravel and explores some terribly
steep canyons. Instead, turn right (east) on Whiskey Run Road.

Seven Devils Road takes its name from how hard it was to cut
a roadway across the seven deep ravines that run at right angles to the
coast south of Cape Arago. Those who explored and hacked away at
the Oregon Coast were apparently often reminded of things satanic.
Already the bike route has passed Devil's Lake, Devil's Punchbowl,
Devil's Churn and Devil's Elbow. Now we get Seven Devils Wayside
and Seven Devils Road. We keep expecting some sort of balance: a
Paradise Park, or a Jesus Loves Us Wayside, or a Heavenly Arch Rock.
No? Continue south on Seven Devils Road.

This tall, prickly shrub at roadside is gorse, or Irish furze. The story goes that Lord Bennett — who founded and named Bandon in 1873 after his home town in County Cork, Ireland — imported gorse to remind him of his homeland. Back in County Cork, native pests keep gorse under control. Here, nothing stops it. Gorse seeds can survive underground for many years. The thorny plant is a fire hazard, too. Oily stalks of gorse helped fuel the fire that leveled Bandon in 1936.

Mile

26.7   Rejoin Highway 101 South.

28.6   Bullards Beach State Park. Hiker/biker campground. The town of Bullards no longer exists. Robert W. Bullard's ferry crossing here was preempted when the Highway 101 bridge crossed the Coquille River. Bullards is best remembered for its high-timin' dance hall, on the second floor of the general store.

Side Trip: Coquille River Lighthouse

From the Highway 101 turnoff to Bullards Beach State Park, it's a three-mile flat bike ride through the park and along the Coquille River to the Coquille River Lighthouse (1896). The lighthouse has been restored but is no longer in use. A change in the river's course shifted the lighthouse from the middle of the river mouth to its present location at the base of the north jetty. The Coquille River Lighthouse holds the embarrassing distinction of having been *hit* by a ship. A schooner rammed the light during a 1903 storm. This and other shipwrecks on the perilous Coquille River Bar are commemorated in a photo exhibit inside the lighthouse.

The trip to the lighthouse and back is short, flat and scenic, unobscured and unprotected by trees or shrubs. If the wind is up, it will get you either coming or going.

Mile

28.9   Cross the Coquille River.

29.4   Turn right off Highway 101 onto lightly-traveled Riverside Drive, to parallel the Coquille River into Bandon.

31.3   Bandon. First and Chicago Streets. Old Town Mall and Port Office. Berth of the *Dixie Lee*, sternwheeler.

BANDON

Bandon is a vital little place that, like gorse but a lot more fun, keeps sprouting new life after fires. Blazes in 1914 and 1936 leveled the town that once supported seven lumber mills at the mouth of the Coquille River. Bandon also sent canned milk, fresh cheese and other farm products to turn-of-the-century San Francisco. Sailing ships rode summer winds to San Francisco in as little as thirty hours, although it might take them six weeks to get back.

Today Bandon is a tourist town. Bandon's Old Town, adjoining the picturesque and active boat basin, has excellent restaurants, vigorous theater and lots of live music to go with the good fishing that brings people to town. Bandon has a wide range of art galleries and crafts shops, and it is home to the best youth hostel on the coast. The spirit of Bandon is perhaps best captured by the entirely whimsical University of Bandon, whose members (teachers are indistinguishable from students) might schedule an inner-tube regatta or a "pre-planned, spontaneous" Ornament Festival. For credit.

Dixie Lee

Treat a weary posterior to a seat on the *Dixie Lee*, a riverboat that paddles up the Coquille River and back to Bandon. The two-hour trip passes Indian village sites and the pilings of ghost towns. This sternwheeler glides through a bird sanctuary and among stands of spruce such as those used for World War II airplanes, including Howard Hughes' *Spruce Goose*. The boat trip narrator is chock full of historical anecdotes, but the best part is when he addresses the on-board piano and bangs out ragtime tunes for the trip back.

Bandon Cheese Factory

On Highway 101 is a factory that produces quality cheddar, Monterey Jack and Colby cheeses. Visitors are welcome to watch the cheese-making through glass windows, and the factory shows a video that covers the process from cow to cheese.

Sea Star Hostel

The hostel, with its International Coffeehouse, is at 375 Second Street in Old Town. Non-members pay more than members but are welcome to share the European-style hosteling experience which includes a common room with wood stove and skylight. Bunk rooms are cozy, sometimes noisy and always clean.

Bandon Historical Museum

The museum, on First Street, is in the building that once housed lifeboat crews of the Coast Guard, which no longer has a station at Bandon. The museum is at its best displaying the rich history of the Coquille Indians, who called themselves Na-So-Mah "the people." Like most other coastal Indians, the Na-So-Mah nurtured themselves at seashore and riverside on abundant fish, clams and crabs. The area also was rich with berries, roots, deer and elk. The natives had little need to practice travel or warfare before Europeans came along. Their basketry is exquisite, and their fishing tools, cooking gear and housing were all well-adapted to wind-blown waterways. The museum has rare pictures of the Indians' sacred Tupper Rock, which no longer exists (see Chapter 8, leaving Bandon). A good little book to go along with the museum's exhibits of Native American culture is *White Moccasins* — a set of stories told to Beverly Ward by her Grandmother Ned, a Coquille Indian.

Beyond native culture, the Bandon museum shows the history of Bullards Bay, the Coquille River Lighthouse, shipwrecks, and the lifesaving station that served the treacherous Coquille River bar. It celebrates the steamship *Elizabeth* that made over six hundred trips to San Francisco before her retirement in 1922.

Each September, Bandon hosts a Cranberry Festival. Along one wall of the museum smile the wonderful pictures of over forty successive Cranberry Festival Queens.

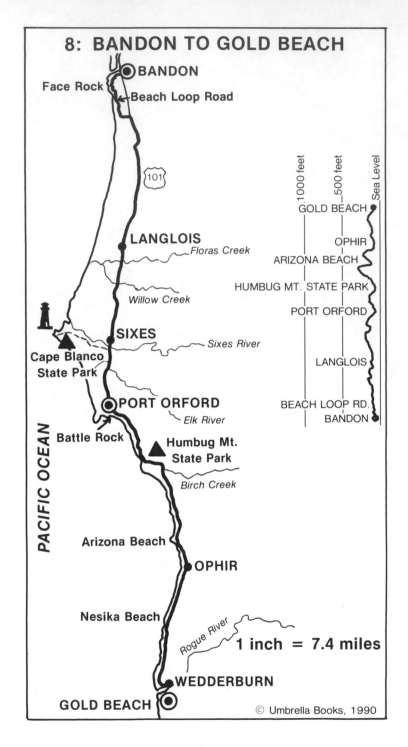

8: BANDON TO GOLD BEACH

BANDON

Face Rock

Beach Loop Road

101

LANGLOIS

Floras Creek

Willow Creek

SIXES

Sixes River

Cape Blanco
State Park

PORT ORFORD

Elk River

Battle Rock

Humbug Mt.
State Park

Birch Creek

PACIFIC OCEAN

Arizona Beach

OPHIR

Nesika Beach

Rogue River

1 inch = 7.4 miles

WEDDERBURN

GOLD BEACH

© Umbrella Books, 1990

1,000 feet — 500 feet — Sea Level

GOLD BEACH
OPHIR
ARIZONA BEACH
HUMBUG MT. STATE PARK
PORT ORFORD
LANGLOIS
BEACH LOOP RD.
BANDON

Chapter 8

BANDON TO GOLD BEACH

(56 Miles)

This leg of the trip starts with a scenic loop along the bluff south of Bandon, with views of the legendary Face Rock, sea stacks and beach. After about five miles, the bike route rejoins Highway 101. Then comes a relatively long, flat and easy ride past cranberry bogs and myrtlewood shops toward historic Port Orford and its Battle Rock, the half-way point.

At Port Orford, the ocean reappears. The surf is within view of the highway for most of the way to Gold Beach. The longest climb of the day comes when Highway 101 cuts around the back side of Humbug Mountain. This is a gradual pull that reaches only about 300 feet in elevation. Shorter ups and downs open to the kind of sea views that appear in coffee-table books about the Oregon coast.

From Ophir to Gold Beach, the last twelve miles, the course flattens out. The route runs parallel to open, sandy beach until it crosses the Rogue River and enters Gold Beach.

Mile

0.0   Bandon at Old Town, First and Chicago Streets. Take First Street west and follow its left turn up the hill to Fourth Street. Turn right. Fourth Street becomes Ocean Drive, which then becomes Seventh Street.

0.4   The remains of Tupper Rock. A low, white wooden fence on the right, opposite 1075 Seventh Street, separates the road from a rock quarry. On the site of this quarry — now just rubble and rock stub — once stood Tupper Rock, a monolith that rose one hundred feet above the current height of the bluff. The rock was sacred to the Coquille Indians, who knew it as Grandmother Rock. Made of a dense and compact stone called blue schist, Tupper Rock was also just about perfect, and conveniently located, for jetty-making. Between 1904 and 1906, the rock was blasted away and redistributed horizontally as the Coquille River's South Jetty.

In 1954 the federal government stripped the Coquille Indians, like many other coastal Indians, of their tribal status. The idea was to welcome Indians into "mainstream" American culture. Most Indian leaders are now of the opinion that it wasn't a very good idea, and the 1980s saw a widespread and successful legal struggle among Native Americans to reconstitute their tribes. The Coquilles were among the last coastal groups to regain their tribal status, in 1989. Since then, the Coquilles have signed an option with the Port of Bandon, which owns the Tupper Rock quarry, to build an Indian museum at their traditional ceremonial site.

Continue on Seventh Street, which soon bends left along the ocean and becomes Beach Loop Drive.

1.9   Face Rock Viewpoint. An Indian legend of Face Rock tells of an innocent maiden who visited this area for a potlatch, a big feast and gift exchange. She had never before seen the ocean. Failing to heed warnings about an evil spirit out there, she got carried away with the beauty of the place and went for a moonlight swim. The evil spirit grabbed her and tried to make her look at him. She wouldn't. Instead, she kept staring at the friendly moon. Face Rock, off shore, preserves in stone this fair maiden's face, in profile. She still gazes hopefully at the moon.

5.4   Rejoin Highway 101 South.

10.4   The terraced and low-diked fields near the road are cranberry bogs. The area south of Bandon and around Langlois is good for growing cranberries because of the acid soil, plentiful water supply and mild winters. Harvest begins toward the end of September, when growers flood the bogs about knee-deep. A beater-machine stirs the water and dislodges the brilliant red berries, which float to the top for easy collection. Although Lewis and Clark noted in their journals that cranberries grew wild on the Oregon coast, the commercial cranberries grown here are an introduced variety. In 1885, Charles Dexter McFarlin failed at panning for gold, so he ordered some cranberry vines from his native Cape Cod. The first bogs on the Oregon coast were built and planted by Chinese laborers. Most Oregon farmers today belong to Ocean Spray, the national cranberry growers' cooperative.

The other exotic growing thing along this stretch of coast is the myrtle tree. Myrtlewood, a fine-grained hardwood, polishes up to a many-shaded luster that some people find attractive as wall clocks and fruit bowls. Local shop owners claim that the myrtle tree grows only here and in the Holy Land. The supposed rarity of myrtlewood would seem to be at odds with the number of myrtlewood shops along this stretch of Highway 101. They're everywhere. Stop and look, before they run out of myrtlewood.

Mile

15.5   Langlois (LANG-loyce). A market and the Greasy Spoon Cafe.

16.4   Cross Floras Creek.

18.2   Cross Willow Creek.

81

23.4   Sixes. A river, a post office and a store. The name comes not from a poker hand or another reference to satan but from the Indian word *sikhs*, for "friend."

24.3   Turnoff to Cape Blanco State Park. Cape Blanco has a hiker/biker campground, but it's over five miles from Highway 101, with a steep climb at the end. The Cape Blanco Lighthouse, the westernmost light in the forty-eight contiguous states and a much-photographed beauty, is closed to the public. Continue on Highway 101.

25.2   Cross the Elk River.

27.7   Enter Port Orford.

28.9   Port Orford. Battle Rock Park.

PORT ORFORD

When the British Captain George Vancouver sighted what we now call Cape Blanco, in 1792, he named it Cape Orford after his friend, George, Earl of Orford. The name didn't stick to the cape, but it slid south to this wind-sheltered cove, where early sailing vessels waited out Pacific storms.

Port Orford, established in 1851, bills itself as the oldest townsite on the Oregon coast. Astoria and Gardiner, by that reckoning, are not on the coast, which is stretching it but technically correct. But let's not quibble. Early settlers were drawn to Port Orford by gold fever and accessible forests, which included wonderful stands of the light, strong and beautiful wood that became known as Port Orford cedar.

Unlike most other significant coastal towns, Port Orford has no river. Its harbor is on the sea, nestled into a nook of shoreline protected from north winds. This harbor gives Port Orford's fishing fleet the advantage of having no dangerous bar to cross. Many of the boats, when in port, get hoisted onto rubber-tired trailers on the docks to avoid sea-battering.

Battle Rock

In June 1851, Captain William Tichenor, who commanded the steamer *Sea Gull* on its rounds between the Columbia River and San Francisco, tried to establish a port of commerce at Port Orford. Tichenor dropped anchor to send an advance party of nine men ashore in small boats. Tichenor's plan was to return from San Francisco in two weeks. The men, eyeing Indians on the beach, refused to leave the *Sea Gull* until Tichenor let them take the ship's cannon.

Hostilities began on June 10, 1851. Indians laid siege to the advance party's camp on the seashore monolith now called Battle Rock. In the next two weeks a reported seventeen Indians died, mostly by cannon fire. When Tichenor and the *Sea Gull* failed to return on time, the advance party, intact but low on food and ammunition, fled up the coast to a white settlement on the Umpqua River. In their absence, Tichenor came back to Port Orford, saw the battle signs and feared his party had been wiped out. The *Sea Gull* steamed on to Portland, where Tichenor heard about his men's escape. With renewed enterprise, he armed and outfitted over sixty men and returned on July 14, 1851, to build a blockhouse and establish his settlement.

Battle Rock is approachable from the beach. A foot trail leads to the top, with a fantastic view of broken coast.

Mile

31.1   Viewpoint back toward Port Orford.

34.6   Humbug Mountain State Park. Hiker/biker campground. The name comes from one of Captain Tichenor's 1851 exploring parties. The men got confused and lost, or "humbugged," in the neighborhood.

CAUTION: As Highway 101 leaves the seashore and cuts to the rear of Humbug Mountain, the road follows the curves of Brush Creek and seems to forget about bikers. The shoulder narrows. Be alert for fallen rock, which collects in the bike lane.

35.3   The shoulder widens again.

36.5   Start a gradual 1.2-mile climb.

37.7   Road summit. The next seven miles or so include some of the most thrilling scenery on the entire coast. The road drops and climbs, drops again and climbs, in full view of the Pacific at its most rugged and grand. Have the camera loaded and ready.

Another thing a biker might notice, in addition to spectacular views, is that the highway itself has a hard time clinging to the United States. The road has sunken grades and unengineered humps and dips, layers of multi-colored asphalt, crumbling roadside cuts and shoulders that want to crack off and fall oceanward. This land is not finished. The coast is still defining itself. It moves, it shifts, it slides each winter as the ocean keeps cutting away.

One stormy night in 1972, Ron Crook, a Gold Beach resident, was riding down the hill north of Arizona Beach in a Datsun station wagon. The road ahead was undermined and, well ... just gone. The Datsun, with Crook and three others in it, plunged into an abyss. Crook was the least-injured passenger (one died). He emerged from the car in time to hear screeching tires and to see another car dive into the pit, on top of the Datsun. "I got a gal out of that second car," says Crook, who then clawed his way up the slick clay cut toward jagged asphalt. He flagged down a truck that was headed for the same hole. "What a nightmare," says Crook, who now works at the Curry County Fairgrounds. "The road was just gone." He adds, with remarkable under-statement: "You really have to watch it, driving these roads in winter."

In summertime, the road tends to stay in place. The wonder here is not that the shoulder isn't always wide or isn't in perfect shape but that it's as good as it is for biking. Instead of cursing the Oregon Department of Transportation, a biker might offer a moment of silent thanks that a route so beautiful and dynamic has room for bikers at all.

41.0   Arizona Beach.

44.7   Cross Euchre Creek. First Ophir exit.

46.2   Second Ophir exit. Too weird to be ignored is the Honey Bear
        RV Park and Campground. In spite of its name, this is a genuine
        German sausage factory. Its Black Forest Kitchen serves only
        evening meals, and reservations are required. German-born
        Gary Saks and his Ecuadorian-born wife Jeannett, migrated to
        Ophir from Los Angeles in 1980. They bought a rundown and
        vandalized campground, spruced it up, built the sausage kitchen
        and lodge, and opened for business three years later. The
        kitchen serves family-style meals near a dance floor that thumps
        with oompah music every night but Monday. Bikers may find it
        difficult, because Honey Bear has not gone undiscovered. The
        RV park caters to mobile condominiums, the kind that are
        pulled by Mercedes and BMWs. Honey Bear is as clean and rich
        as a country club, with the women well-coiffed and the men apt
        to wear lemon slacks. But a section of the campground is
        reserved for tents, and the sausage is *wunderbar*, the beer
        ausgezeichnet.

        To get there, leave Highway 101 at the second Ophir exit. Take
        the frontage road (Curry County Road 510) half a mile south.

55.4   Rogue River Bridge. Completed in 1931 and dedicated in 1932,
        the bridge is one of C.B. McCullough's earliest and most beauti-
        ful. It helped connect Gold Beach and Brookings to the rest of
        the state, though the automobile trip up the coast still involved
        ferry crossings at the major rivers and estuaries.

55.7   Entering Gold Beach.

GOLD BEACH

        The overflow of eager humanity into the California gold rush of
1849 reached the Oregon Country in the early 1850s. The first prospectors arrived at the mouth of the Rogue River in 1852 and found easy
pickings. They found flakes of gold in the dark sandy beaches, and they
found pay streaks in ocean-facing bluffs. The prospectors then took
their pans and rockers and sluice boxes up the nearby rivers in search
of ledges and veins that were the source of this beachside gold.

Newspaper accounts include stories such as the miner who shipped a single gold-filled boulder, worth $2,700, to San Francisco.

Right on the heels of this frenetic and rude influx came "civilization," mainly those who supplied the miners and who had every reason to encourage gold fever. The gold deposits, though rich, were soon exhausted. Major storms of the winter of 1854 buried the gold sands and brought home to the miners just how difficult it would be to sustain their claims on the beach. As if that weren't enough, the Rogue River Indians met these greedy newcomers with hostilities that soon stretched from Port Orford in the north to the Chetco River in the south. Many separate uprisings became known collectively as the Rogue River Indian Wars of 1855 and 1856.

Once the Army got a grip on things, more people got rich from timber and salmon than from gold. Today, Gold Beach is strongly positioned to mine tourist money. It's a good place to part with some money. The beaches and seascapes are beautiful. There are excellent runs of salmon and steelhead into the Rogue, and the Rogue River itself has some of the finest whitewater rafting and wilderness areas in the Pacific Northwest. Portions of the river, which was a familiar haunt of novelist Zane Grey, have been designated a National Wild and Scenic River.

Highway 101 through town is Ellensburg Avenue. The town itself was initially called Ellensburg, after one of Captain Tichenor's daughters, Sarah Ellen. Because the name was easily confused with another Ellensburg, in Washington Territory, it was changed to the more descriptively alluring Gold Beach.

Rogue River Jet Boats

For those not averse to powering through wilderness, Rogue River jet boats are the easy way to experience sensational scenery. Shallow-draft boats, some with more than a thousand horsepower of hydrojet, skim the rapids and carry up to two dozen passengers at a time into the back country. The pilots give a running commentary on the geography and history of the river, and it's not at all unusual on these trips to see bald eagle, beaver and deer.

Round trips vary in length from 64 to 104 miles. The shorter trips are available twice daily. Two outfits provide jet-boat excursions: Jerry's Rogue Jets depart from near the south side of the Rogue River Bridge, and Mail Boat hydrojets depart from near the north end of the bridge. The mail boat does, in fact, deliver mail as well as tourists to the town of Agnes and points inland.

Rogue-Pacific Interpretive Center

This private, nonprofit learning center, at 510 Colvin Street (one block off Highway 101, behind the Curry County Courthouse), charges a modest fee for one- or two-day workshops on the area's natural and unnatural history. Find out, for example, what's lurking and crawling around in the tidepools, how to find and dig clams or what happened to the early gold mines of Curry County. Call 247-2732 for short-course descriptions and times.

Curry County Museum

At 920 Ellensburg Ave. (Highway 101), the museum has good old pictures of the construction and dedication of the Rogue River Bridge. Reproduced inside the museum is the interior of a gold miner's cabin, with tools of the trade. At least as informative as the exhibits is the museum manager, Mildred Walker. She's a live wire who has lived in Pistol River since 1946 and who loves to talk about local history.

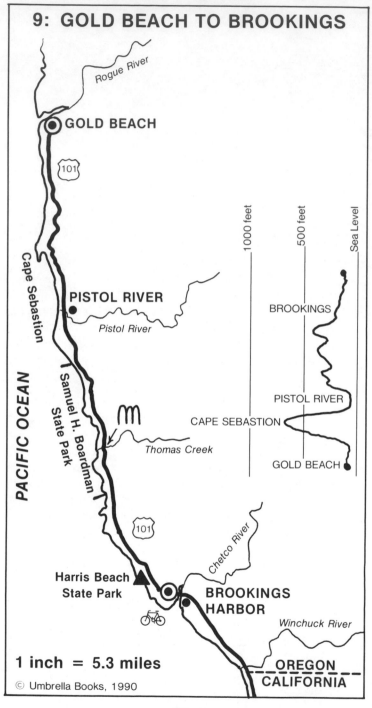

9: GOLD BEACH TO BROOKINGS

Chapter 9

GOLD BEACH TO BROOKINGS

(31 Miles)

The coastal bike route saves some of the best scenery for last, but bikers have to work for it. Today's wake-up call is the climb out of Gold Beach and over the hump of Cape Sebastian. This three-mile ascent reaches an elevation of 700 feet, the highest point on Highway 101 between Washington and California.

The bike route follows Highway 101 all day. The road descends south of Cape Sebastian to run flat for six miles. Sea stacks rise from the ocean on the right, and the meadows of Pistol River country lie on the left.

Then come a dozen or so up-and-down miles that include some of the most gorgeous and pristine spots on the Oregon coast. Samuel H. Boardman State Park is a linear park, bounded by the Pacific on the west and Highway 101 on the east. Viewpoints along the way overlook towering cliffs, sheltered coves, rock arches and natural bridges.

Carry liquids and food. There are great picnic spots but no grocery stores on Highway 101 between Gold Beach and Brookings.

Brookings and its neighboring town, Harbor, are the southern-most population center in the state. From there the road goes flat for five more miles to the California border. Crescent City, California, is nineteen miles beyond the state line.

Mile

0.0   Gold Beach, at Rogue River Bridge.

2.0   Leaving Gold Beach.

2.8   Start the three-mile climb up Cape Sebastian. On January 20, 1603, Sebastian Vizcaino sailed north from Mexico and named a prominent headland at 42 degrees latitude after his patron saint, whose feast was celebrated on that day. Later Vizcaino's recorded latitudes were determined to have been in error, too high. So it is not entirely clear that today's Cape Sebastian is the same cape that Vizcaino saw, but the name was fixed to this feature by U.S. survey teams in 1869.

5.7   Road summit.

11.2   Cross the Pistol River. James Mace fumbled his pistol and lost it in the river in 1853, thereby giving the river a name that stuck.

       In March of 1856 a big Indian fight raged for several days near the present site of the Pistol River Bridge. A company of over thirty Minutemen, on their way north to join in the Rogue River Indian Wars, got pinned here with their backs to the sea. Surrounded on three sides, the volunteers hastily constructed a shelter of driftwood logs and engaged the Indians in close combat. The siege was finally broken when regular troops arrived from Crescent City and dispersed the Indians. A reported seventeen Indians and one soldier died.

11.9   Turnoff to the townsite of Pistol River, just a grocery store now, three quarters of a mile off Highway 101 on the old coast road.

16.3   Enter Boardman State Park. No camping. The next ten miles border an elongated coastline park, between the highway and spectacular ocean scenery. Samuel H. Boardman (1874-1953), was a highway engineer and nature lover from Lowell, Massachusetts. He made his way to Oregon in 1903 and began working for the Oregon State Highway Department in 1916. A champion of roadside improvements and park development,

Boardman became superintendent of the highway department in 1929. His vision and energy in that post earned him the title, "Father of Oregon State Parks." Boardman persuaded the state to buy this particular awe-inspiring stretch of coast in 1950, on the eve of his retirement.

16.9   Arch Rock Point. Viewpoint.

18.0   Thunder Rock Cove. Viewpoint.

18.1   Natural Bridges Cove. Viewpoint. All of the viewpoints in Boardman State Park are good, but don't miss this one. Walk thirty yards to a wooden-deck overlook. Far below, waves burst through the rock arches and fan into green tidal pools.

19.9   Thomas Creek Bridge. At 345 feet, this bridge is higher than the Golden Gate Bridge and the tallest in Oregon. If you dare, look down between sheer cliffs at the tiny trickle of Thomas Creek, which sliced this horrendous gash to the sea. The bridge is recent, built in 1963. Before then, the coastal route wound inland from Pistol River to Brookings, a trip by car that took forty-five minutes and now takes twenty minutes.

Mildred Walker, a Pistol River resident who drives a Brookings school bus and manages the Curry County Museum in Gold Beach, has good reason to appreciate the new road. She remembers the construction of Thomas Creek Bridge. The three-year project was nearly finished, in 1962, when an elderly couple motored up from Brookings to take a look.

"A little old man and his wife," says Walker, "were out for a Sunday drive. The man drove onto some loose one-by-twelve planks on the unfinished deck of the bridge. Once he got out there and saw where he was, he was afraid to back off," Walker says. "They stayed in the car all Sunday afternoon, Sunday night, and a wind came up. They must have been terrified, petrified," she says. "Finally the workmen got there on Monday morning and hauled them off the bridge."

21.9 Whalehead Viewpoint. A massive rock offshore lies in the shape of a beached whale.

23.4 House Rock Viewpoint. Look north for an overview of the wild coastline just traveled.

25.5 Leaving Boardman State Park.

27.6 Entering Brookings.

28.0 Harris Beach State Park. A quarter mile from Highway 101 is the hiker/biker campground, with easy access to sandy beach, rocky outcroppings and tidepools. On the opposite side of Highway 101 from the park is the Oregon State Highway Department's Tourist Information Center.

30.0 Turnoff to Azalea State Park, a quarter of a mile to the left and up a short hill. Dedicated by Samuel Boardman in 1939, the twenty-three-acre park has corridors of the fragrant pink and creamy-white native azaleas that open onto grassy glades and lead among tall trees. From April into June is the high season for azaleas, but the park is a nice resting and picnicking spot all year. Day use only.

30.2 Chetco River Bridge, with a commanding view of the Port of Brookings and the river mouth.

31.0 Brookings-Harbor Visitor Information Center.

BROOKINGS-HARBOR

Chetco Indians populated the flat land between the Chetco and Winchuck Rivers when Jedediah Smith and his trapper band trudged through in 1828. By 1852 a coastal land route from California brought more trappers, miners and packers into the area. A.F. Miller was one of twelve men who settled that year at the mouth of the Chetco. For a while things went peaceably between settlers and Indians, but a report of the Commissioner of Indian Affairs for 1854 states that Miller, with several accomplices, burned Indian dwellings and killed fifteen Chetcos because these Indians were giving free canoe rides and interfering with the profits of Miller's ferry. Miller was arrested and brought to Port Orford, where the authorities held him for six weeks and then set him free "for want of sufficient evidence."

Miller's alleged attack brought on a period of off-and-on hostilities that melded into the Rogue River Indian Wars. At the mouth of the Chetco, in May of 1856, Indians ambushed an Army pack train on its way from Crescent City to Rogue River to subdue Indian bands.

After the Army brought peace to the area, agriculture dominated the flatlands south of the Chetco River in the late nineteenth century. In 1913, Brookings was founded on the other side of the river. It was named after Robert S. Brookings, the major stockholder in a huge lumbering venture.

Not until 1922 was a railroad bridge built across the Chetco. Automobiles began crossing on a steel bridge four years later. A news item in the July 7, 1927, *Gold Beach Reporter* celebrates the opening of the Roosevelt Highway between Pistol River and Brookings: "It has not been graveled and is rough in spots, but it is a great improvement over the old mountain trail that has been used for so many years." Brookings was no longer "cut off" from the rest of the state.

The stunner in all this is how late the Brookings area developed and how thin Oregon coastal history really is. Imagine your outstretched arm as a time line, starting at the shoulder with Vizcaino's 1603 cruise off the southern Oregon coast. Captains James Cook and Robert Gray and Lewis and Clark are all bunched about your elbow. Brookings was not founded until about your wrist. The paved coastal highway came only about three generations (or knuckles) ago.

Today the adjoining towns of Brookings and Harbor are separated only by the emerald calm of the Chetco River, an important commercial and sport fishing outlet. The Chetco River bar is among the smoothest on the Oregon coast, allowing ocean access to boats as small as fourteen feet long. Since the jetties (1957) and the new boat basin (1960) were finished, as many as 12,000 boats cross the Chetco River Bar each August.

Because winter temperatures are higher here than at other Oregon coast ports, and because year-round temperatures are seldom extreme, Brookings bills itself as "The Banana Belt" of the Oregon coast. Brookings-Harbor is a popular and still-growing retirement spot. Flowers bloom all year. The mild winters, gently-sloping fields and rich, slightly acidic soils make the area ideal for cultivating bulbs. Lilies do especially well. Over ninety percent of the total U.S. lily crop is grown in Curry County and California's adjoining Del Norte County.

Brookings' biggest annual civic bash is the Azalea Festival. It has been celebrated in late May or early June for over fifty years, since the dedication of Azalea State Park in 1939.

Chetco Valley Museum

The museum is within view of Highway 101, 2.6 miles south of the Brookings-Harbor Visitor Information Center. Turn left on Museum Road. The museum exhibits a fine collection of pioneer artifacts, but the chief attraction is the small red building that houses it, Blake House. Harrison Blake, a rancher, was Curry County's first deputy sheriff and first representative to the state legislature. Blake built the home in 1857, and it is said to be the area's oldest standing house. On one corner of the grounds towers the world's largest known Monterey Cypress, 27 feet in diameter.

Oregon/California Border

Compulsive types won't want to quit the Oregon coast until they have stepped on a piece of California, which starts a mere 4.5 miles south of the Brookings-Harbor Visitor Information Center. The route to the state line is conveniently flat and open, skirting fertile fields where they grow the lilies. Welcome to California, 370 miles from the start of the Oregon coast bike route in Astoria. Come back soon.

Appendices

I. Getting Back

Like drifting a river, the bike ride down the coast presents the the problem of getting back to the starting point. Many bikers will continue south to San Francisco. Biking back up Highway 101 and into the wind is no fun, but there are several options.

The best option is to arrange to be met by a loved one in Brookings, and load the bike onto his/her car. But if the loved one also needs a ride back, the bus may be the best option. Greyhound has a San Francisco-to-Portland line that passes through Brookings twice daily. The bus retraces the coastal bike route north to Lincoln City, then turns inland to Portland. Bikes must be boxed. The Escape Hatch bike shop in Brookings often has bike boxes, or check at the local Coast to Coast Store.

For those with the time and the inclination to see more of Oregon, it is possible — not easy — to loop inland and back north. This is done by heading south into California on Highway 101, and then taking Highway 199 North to Grants Pass. Watch out for a very narrow and dangerous section of Highway 199 along California's Smith River, between Patrick Creek and the tunnel at the California-Oregon border. The best way to tackle this section is to hitch a ride in a pickup truck, and bypass it. Biking from Grants Pass to Crater Lake (elevation 8,000 feet), is as scenic as it is strenuous. Highway 97 North, on the east side of the Cascades, has a wide shoulder and is less windy than the coast. It's a good way to experience "the other" Oregon, the high desert.

From Reedsport, there are two ways to get to Eugene and connect to Willamette Valley bike routes back to Portland. The Smith River Road is lightly traveled — dotted with campgrounds but lacking towns and stores. Highway 38, along the Umpqua River and through Scottsburg, Drain and Cottage Grove, has more traffic but good shoulder most of the way. Both routes are scenic, and both are demanding, because they cross the Coast Range at elevations up to 1,500 feet.

II. Visitor Information

The state of Oregon publishes biking maps called "Oregon Coast Bike Route" and "Oregon Bicycling Guide." The latter includes nearly all of Oregon's 7,600 miles of state highways, color-coded to show their suitability for bicycle travel. Contact the Bicycle Program Manager, Oregon Department of Transportation, Room 200, Transportation Building, Salem, Oregon 97310. The phone number is (503) 378-3432. (503) 373-7455.

The offices listed below are ready sources of information about things to do and places to stay on the Oregon Coast.

Regional Associations

Oregon Tourism Division   in Oregon: 1-800-233-3306
595 Cottage Street NE   outside Oregon: 1-800-547-7842
Salem, OR 97310

Oregon State Parks   (503) 238-7488
525 Trade Street SE
Salem, OR 97310

Oregon Lodging Association   (503) 255-5135
12624 Stark Street
Portland, OR 97233

Oregon Coast Association   (503) 336-5107
P.O. Box 670   in Oregon: 1-800-982-6278
Newport, OR 97365

RA2 TRANSPO 325 5641

Sun 5PM CHAMBE of Comerce

Local Organizations

Chapter	Office	Phone
√1	Astoria Area Visitor Center 111 W. Marine Drive Astoria, OR 97103	(503) 325-6311
1	Seaside Visitor Bureau Highway 101 and Broadway in Oregon: Seaside, OR 97138	(503) 738-6391 1-800-444-6740
√1&2	Cannon Beach Chamber of Commerce Second and Spruce Cannon Beach, OR 97110	(503) 436-2623
2	Garibaldi Chamber of Commerce Highway 101 and Second Street Garibaldi, OR 97118	(503) 322-0301
√2&3	Tillamook County Visitor Center 3705 Highway 101 North Tillamook, OR 97141	(503) 842-7525
√3	Pacific City/Woods Chamber of Commerce Box 331 Pacific City, OR 97135	(503) 965-6161
4	Lincoln City Visitor Center 3939 NW Highway 101 in Oregon: Lincoln City, OR 97367	(503) 994-3070 1-800-452-2151
4	Depoe Bay Chamber of Commerce 214 SE Highway 101 Depoe Bay, OR 97341	(503) 765-2889
√4&5	Greater Newport Visitor Center 555 SW Coast Highway (101) Newport, OR 97365	(503) 265-8801

5   Waldport Visitor Center   (503) 563-2133
Highway 101
Waldport, OR 97394

5   Yachats Chamber of Commerce   (503) 547-3530
Highway 101 and 2d Street
Yachats, OR 97498

✓ 5&6   Florence Area Visitor Center   (503) 997-3128
Highway 101
Florence, OR 97439

6   Lower Umpqua Visitor Center   (503) 271-3495
Highways 101 and 38
Reedsport, OR 97467

6&7   North Bend Information Center   (503) 756-4613
1380 Sherman (Hwy 101)
North Bend, OR 97459

6&7   Bay Area Visitor Center   (503) 269-0215
50 E. Central (Hwy 101)   in Oregon: 1-800-762-6278
Coos Bay, OR 97240   outside Oregon: 1-800-824-8486

7   Charleston Visitor Center   (503) 888-2311
Cape Arago Highway
Charleston, OR 97420

7&8   Bandon Visitor Centor   (503) 347-9616
350 Second Street
Bandon, OR 97411

8   Port Orford Chamber of Commerce   (503) 332-8055
PO Box 637
Port Orford, OR 97465

8&9   Gold Beach-Wedderburn Visitor Center   (503) 247-7526
510 S. Ellensburg   in Oregon: 1-800-452-2334
Gold Beach, OR 97444

9   Brookings-Harbor Visitor Center   (503) 469-3181
Highway 101 South-Harbor
Brookings, OR 97415

III. Bicycle Repair Shops

(Arranged From North To South)

Astoria (97103)
  Hauer's Cyclery   (503) 325-7334
  1606 Marine Drive

Seaside (97138)
  Prom Bike Shop   (503) 738-8251
  325 S. Holladay

Cannon Beach (97110)
  Mike's Bike Shop   (503) 436-1266
  248 N. Spruce

Tillamook (97141)
  Drake's Bike & Mower   (503) 842-2783
  2506 Third Street

Otis (97368)
  Kats Bike Repair   (503) 994-5242
  5655 N. Highway 101

Newport (97365)
  Newport Schwinn Cyclery (503) 265-8000
  644 SW Coast Highway (101)

Waldport (97394)
  R's Bicycle Repair   (503) 563-5062
  901 Wazivata Avenue

Florence (97439)
      Spokes-N-Stuff   (503) 997-2735
      549 Highway 101

Reedsport (97467)
      Oliver Bradford Bike Repairs   (503) 271-4624
      678 W. Alder Place

North Bend (97459)
      Moe's   (503) 756-7536
      1397 Sherman Avenue

      Bay Area Bike Center   (503) 756-4522
      2261 Newmark

Brookings (97415)
      Escape Hatch   (503) 469-2914
      656 Chetco Avenue

IV. RECOMMENDED READING

Historical References:

Astoria, by Washington Irving. Donohue, Henneberry, 1936.

Reach of Tide, Ring of History: A Columbia River Voyage, by Sam McKinney. Oregon Historical Society, 1987.

The Journals of Lewis and Clark, edited by Bernard A. DeVoto. Houghton Mifflin, 1953.

A History of Oregon, by Robert C. Clark. Row, Peterson, 1931.

Oregon Geographic Names, by Lewis L. McArthur. Oregon Historical Society, 1974.

Historic Highway Bridges of Oregon, by Dwight A. Smith. Oregon Historical Society, 1986.

Roadside Geology of Oregon, by David D. Alt and Donald W. Hyndman. Mountain Press, 1978.

Pioneer History of Coos and Curry Counties, Oregon, by Orville Dodge. Curry Pioneer and Historical Assn., 1969.

Stories:

Trask, by Don Berry. Viking, 1960.

To Build a Ship, by Don Berry. Viking, 1964.

Sometimes a Great Notion, by Ken Kesey. Penguin Books, 1964.

The River Why, by David James Duncan. Bantam Books, 1983.

Top Deck Twenty! Best West Coast Sea Stories! by Stan Allyn. Binford & Mort, 1989.

White Moccasins, by Beverly Ward. Myrtle Point Printing, 1986.

Biking:

Bicycling the Pacific Coast, by Tom Kirkendall and Vicky Spring. The Mountaineers, 1984.

Touring on Two Wheels: The Bicycle Traveler's Handbook, by Dennis Coello. Lyons & Burford, 1985.

Richard's New Bicycle Book, by Richard Ballantine. Ballantine Books, 1987.

Oregon Coast Food and Lodging

Northwest Best Places, by David Brewster and Kathryn Robinson. Sasquatch Books, 1987.

Bed & Breakfast Northwest, by Myrna Oakley. Solstice Press, 1984.

Index

About the Author

Robin Cody was born in 1943 at St. Helens, Oregon, and was raised in Estacada, Oregon. His father was an avid fisherman and his mother an Oregon history nut, so Cody became familiar early with the coastal rivers and the stories of explorers and early inhabitants of the Oregon Coast. Traveling the coast by bicycle, he was struck by how few bikers knew of coastal lore.

Cody graduated from Yale University and served as a lieutenant in the U.S. Army in Germany. He and his wife, Donna, taught at the American School of Paris for nine years before returning to Oregon, where he became Dean of Admissions at Portland's Reed College.

Cody has made a living since 1983 as a basketball referee, baseball umpire, and free-lance writer. A frequent contributor to *Northwest Magazine* of the *Sunday Oregonian*, Cody won the Silver Spur Award of the Western Writers of America in 1986 for short non-fiction.